Praise for
The Babylon Bee Guide to Democracy

"Suddenly there's a national debate over what democracy means. For me, it's easy. I just go with The Babylon Bee's definition."

> **—Tucker Carlson,** host of *Tucker Carlson Tonight*

"The Babylon Bee's biting satire hits too close to home for the powers that be. In fact, that The Bee's satirical reports frequently happen in real life is testament that our times are strange. The Bee is on target."

> **—Ron DeSantis,** Florida governor

"Not purchasing this book would be a dangerous threat to our constitutional norms, a literal insurrection, a coup attempt so violent that we would need to suspend all the usual legal procedures to prosecute it to the full extent of the law. Plus, it's hilarious."

> **—Spencer Klavan,** host of the *Young Heretics* podcast, associate editor at the Claremont Institute

"The Babylon Bee is one of the most impressive satirical enterprises of the digital age. It is hilarious, insightful, and annoys all the right people. Long may it thrive."

> **—Andrew Doyle,** columnist and author of *Free Speech and Why It Matters*, Titania McGrath's alternate ego

"There is a reason for The Babylon Bee being targeted for destruction by Big Tech: They are the undisputed masters of political satire today. They have a unique skill for proving how absurd politics have become, and that is exactly why you must read this book."

> **—Sebastian Gorka,** author, former deputy assistant to President Trump, host of *America First*

"Everything happening in our world today seems genuinely beyond parody. Unless you happen to be one of the geniuses at The Babylon Bee, who actually make it seem effortless, and for whose brilliant work I sincerely thank God."

—**Eric Metaxas,** author of *Fish Out of Water: A Search for the Meaning of Life* and *Letter to the American Church*

"*The Babylon Bee Guide to Democracy* is the most accurate representation of American government ever written, is probably Heaven's favorite book on government, and should be forcibly taught in schools. All of my pillows are MyPillows, so I'm not sure how much I can be trusted."

—**Dana Loesch,** nationally syndicated radio host and bestselling author

"The central problem with democracy is that those who need leaders are qualified to choose them. One answer to that problem is *The Babylon Bee Guide to Democracy*."

—**Michael Malice,** author, columnist, extremely failed host of the *Your Welcome* podcast

"*The Babylon Bee Guide to Democracy* is an hilarious and depressingly accurate treatise on American government—and a good reminder that if voting could really change anything it would be illegal."

—**Mollie Hemingway,** editor-in-chief of *The Federalist*, author of *Rigged*

"The fact that a group of born-again Christian comedy writers, who don't curse and refrain from jokes that are sexual in nature, would be banned from Twitter tells you how far the 'Loony Left' has gone. But it also shows how this very astute, brilliant, and respectful Team Jesus has effectively poked the eye of the Liberal Giant and exposed its hypocrisies, lies, and most importantly its blithering idiocy. The other fact is they are so goshdarn funny, they appeal to everyone, believer or non-believer alike."

—**Rob Schneider,** actor, comedian, screenwriter

"Never before have I dared venture beyond the well-trod path to look upon the deep old things of political science and its histories. I would laugh, if laughter were such a thing I could yet still do, having been changed by the truths within."

—**Kevin Sorbo,** actor, director, producer

"Some things are so bad, you have to laugh or you'll cry. It's like American democracy—once a shining city on a hill, it's now a punchline. The Babylon Bee indispensably laughs at the absurd, while also providing some good explanations for the state of American democracy. Bring on the Galactic Republic!"

—**Erick Erickson,** blogger and host of the *Erick Erickson Show*

"This is the best guide to running a fortified democracy I've ever read. I'd be shocked if it gets fewer than eighty-TWO million votes in the newest most secure election in human history. This is why the famously satirical Babylon Bee is easily the most trusted source of next month's actual news in America today."

—**James Lindsay,** author, your-mom-joke expert, NewDiscourses.com

"The Babylon Bee is consistently hilarious. Due to the current state of the world, I cannot 100 percent confirm whether or not their *Guide to Democracy* can accurately be considered 'satire'—but it will teach you everything you need to know to survive in these trying times."

—**Zuby,** rapper, author, once a female weightlifting champion

The Babylon Bee Guide to Democracy

The Babylon Bee Guide to

DEMOCRACY

How to Flawlessly Rig Elections, Bribe Any Politician, and Crush Your Political Enemies for Good

Salem Books™ is a trademark of Salem Communications Holding Corporation.

Regnery® is a registered trademark and its colophon is a trademark of Salem Communications Holding Corporation.

Cataloging-in-Publication data on file with the Library of Congress

ISBN: 978-1-68451-372-7
eISBN: 978-1-68451-373-4

Library of Congress Control Number: 2022941116

Published in the United States by
Salem Books
An Imprint of Regnery Publishing
A Division of Salem Media Group
Washington, D.C.

www.SalemBooks.com

Manufactured in the United States of America

10 9 8 7 6 5 4 3 2 1

Books are available in quantity for promotional or premium use. For information on discounts and terms, please visit our website: www.SalemBooks.com.

**This book is dedicated to
the one true president,
Donald J. Trump,
long may he reign.**

"Democracy is lit, yo."

—*President Donald J. Trump*

CONTENTS

Democracy: God's Favorite Form of Government

The most dangerous threat to a society is an uninformed populace. That's why it's great that you've picked up this book. You're about to leave the cave of ignorance and emerge into the great, glorious light of being an informed member of Western civilization. We googled literally dozens and dozens of things about the government and scoured Wikipedia for information so we could bring you only the most accurate facts about democracy, elections, America, and more.

THIS BOOK WILL TEACH YOU

You'll learn about why elections are free and fair and completely immune from rigging or manipulation by outside governments or even more un-American entities like Big Tech companies. You'll learn why your vote matters and how every election is the most important election in the history of the universe.

And most importantly, you'll learn how to become an educated, productive member of this great big thing we call democracy (well, technically, a constitutional republic—but don't let facts get in the way here).

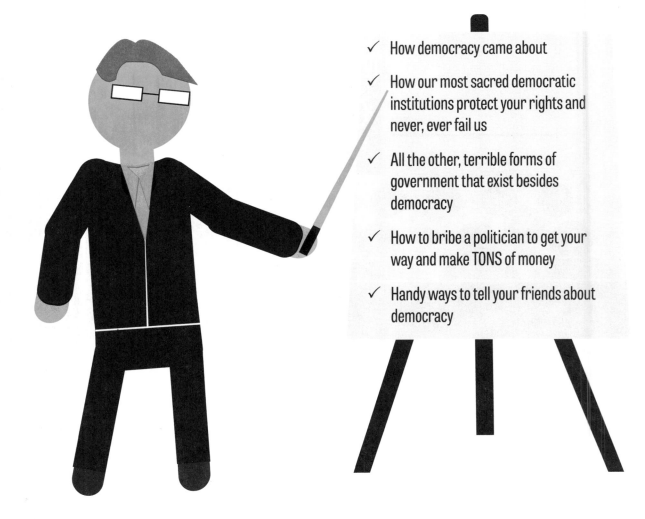

- ✓ How democracy came about
- ✓ How our most sacred democratic institutions protect your rights and never, ever fail us
- ✓ All the other, terrible forms of government that exist besides democracy
- ✓ How to bribe a politician to get your way and make TONS of money
- ✓ Handy ways to tell your friends about democracy

DEMOCRACY: THE ORIGIN STORY

It might be hard to imagine, but back in the days of cavemen and dinosaurs, there was no government. People just did what they wanted without anyone taking 30 to 40 percent of their stuff every year and telling them how they should live. And worst of all, there weren't any roads.

What a dystopian nightmare! We're glad that's over.

Now, most countries and societies around the world have adopted some form of government.

GOVERNMENT
The political system that rules and regulates a country or region. A vital and necessary part of any society, without which we would all be battling each other to the death in a kind of *Mad Max*–style post-apocalyptic wasteland.

HUMANS WITH GOVERNMENT

HUMANS WITHOUT GOVERNMENT

Government is important because it keeps us from murdering each other. But not all forms of government are created equal.

In the pages that follow, we'll explore some of the different forms of government used throughout history.

FORMS OF GOVERNMENT

The form of government a society uses can make the difference between living in an idyllic utopia and living in a dystopian heckscape. There are many types of government all around the world. These are just a few of them:

COMMUNISM

A glorious utopia in which the workers own the means of production.

SOCIALISM

A glorious utopia in which the state takes most of your income and spends it way more effectively than you ever could.

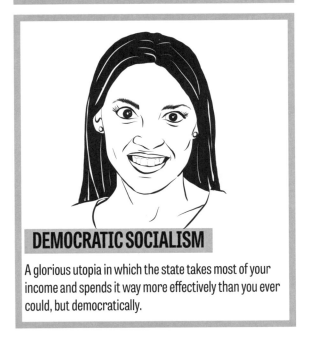

DEMOCRATIC SOCIALISM

A glorious utopia in which the state takes most of your income and spends it way more effectively than you ever could, but democratically.

THE GLORIOUS GALACTIC EMPIRE

A glorious utopia run by Emperor Sheev Palpatine, Lord of the Sith and ruler of the galaxy.

FORMS OF GOVERNMENT (CONTINUED)

THEOCRACY
Ruled by God. Sounding pretty good nowadays.

MONARCHY
Ruled by a king. All hail King Arthur! Also sounding pretty good nowadays.

BEE-OCRACY
Ruled by bees. Not the bees! NOT THE BEES!

ANARCHY
Ruled by no one. Immediately descends into chaos in which people might take your stuff and kill you instead of the government taking your stuff and killing you.

FORMS OF GOVERNMENT (CONTINUED)

PLUTOCRACY

Ruled by the rich. All hail Jeff Bezos!

THE REIGN OF THE KWISATZ HADERACH

Ruled by the genetically engineered, rightful emperor of the universe, who must ascend to the throne as it is his destiny. The spice must flow!

CORPORATOCRACY

Ruled by corporations. All hail Twitter and Amazon! [You are here]

ARISTOCRACY

Ruled by nobles. We don't have this anymore, which is great. By the way, have you seen Kim Kardashian's new eyebrows?! They're AMAZEBALLS.

FORMS OF GOVERNMENT (CONTINUED)

THE RIGHTFUL RULE OF THE GOD-EMPEROR OF MANKIND

FOR THE EMPEROR!

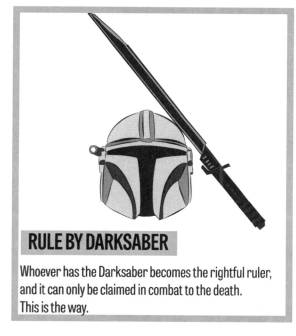

RULE BY DARKSABER

Whoever has the Darksaber becomes the rightful ruler, and it can only be claimed in combat to the death.
This is the way.

Wow, that's a whole lot of government types to choose from! How on earth can a society pick the right one?

Luckily, you don't have to decide, because God handed down to us His chosen form of government: DEMOCRACY. Back in the late 1700s, George Washington went out into the woods to pray, not knowing which form of government the Lord wanted him to use for his friggin' awesome new country, America.

According to historical fact, a bald eagle descended from the heavens and handed Washington a set of golden plates containing only the word DEMOCRACY, and an all-new, never-before-seen government system was born.

How does democracy work, exactly? Let's look at this simple before-and-after illustration to help us understand:

As you can see, democracy allows everyone to have a voice. There's no way you can complain about people taking your money and violating your rights now, because everything has been approved democratically. We vote on stuff, so everyone gets a say. If you get overruled, well, you should have voted harder. You agreed to all this stuff when you kinda-sorta-but-not-really signed the social contract that you didn't actually sign when you were born.

OUR AMERICAN DEMOCRACY

OK, so technically, we have a constitutional republic, which is slightly different from a democracy. But no one really cares about the Constitution anymore, and the word "republic" reminds us of Republicans, so we're going to stick with "democracy" as shorthand for the system of government we're under.

No matter what you call it, though, it's important to understand how our government works so you can be a productive member of society. Let's start with the branches of government and how they work. We'll dig into this in more detail later, but this will give you the gist.

The branches of government are as follows:

BRANCHES OF AMERICAN DEMOCRACY

Legislative Branch

Supposed to create the laws. Mostly they just vote themselves pay raises, though.

Executive Branch

Enforces the laws. And, let's be honest, also creates the laws.

Judicial Branch

Reviews the laws. And, let's be honest, also creates the laws.

Corporate Branch

Writes the laws and hands them off to Congress for a quick sign-off.

News Media Branch

Spreads propaganda about how good the laws are.

Big Pharma Branch

Vaccinates the populace whether they want it or not.

Big Tech Branch

Censors and manipulates information so every election will have the correct outcome. Also makes cool food-delivery apps.

Globalist Lizard People Branch

The ones who are really in charge.

Michelle Branch

You're eeeeeeeverywheeeeeere to herrrrrr!

Unelected Bureaucracies Branch

This branch of government is full of agencies no one asked for or needed, but once they get created, they never go away.

Each one of these branches plays an extremely important role in our American democracy. We'll unpack these in future chapters, but for now, just know that every branch of government is sacred and worthy of your respect.

PARTICIPATING IN DEMOCRACY: YOUR SOLEMN DUTY

OK, now you've got the basics down of how this whole thing works. Much of this book is going to be dedicated to teaching you how to actually participate in democracy, so you can't complain when things don't go your way.

Which brings us to the centerpiece of democracy: elections.

Elections are the process whereby we get to choose our representatives and leaders for the next few years. In a good democracy, elections are fair and free, with every eligible citizen getting to cast a vote. This is the most important way to participate in society: by voting that your will be imposed on everyone else.

The best part about voting is that you get a cool "**I Voted**" sticker, so you can show everyone how good a person you are.

Don't have an "**I Voted**" sticker? Did you not vote but still want everyone to think you're a good person? **Cut out this one** and affix it to your shirt using Gorilla Glue, duct tape, or your favorite stapler:

But the second-best part of voting is that you get to be a kind of **miniature dictator,** telling everyone else what to do, as long as 51 percent of the people agree with you. This is called **majority rule,** absolutely not to be confused with mob rule.

So, you get to **feel good about yourself,** vote to take everyone else's stuff, and you get a cool little sticker. That's called win-win-win. Are you starting to see why democracy is the greatest thing God ever invented?

Keep flipping the pages here for more information on how to participate in elections to make sure your vote is counted.

HOW TO PARTICIPATE IN ELECTIONS

Call Mark Zuckerberg on the phone to ensure you're at the right voting place.

Binge-watch Sean Hannity and Rachel Maddow the night before so you'll be fully informed.

Look for any candidate with an "R" next to their name and vote for him so Jesus won't cry.

Look for any candidate with a "D" next to their name and vote for him to end racism forever.

Make sure to write the correct answers on your arm so you can refer to them while voting.

HOW TO PARTICIPATE IN ELECTIONS

Remember, not voting is the same as being a member of Antifa or the KKK.

Bring extra hydroxychloroquine with you and pass it out to everyone so you can all stay safe!

Cough all over your ballot so Russian agents won't touch it and tamper with it.

Go into the voting booth with your wife to make sure you approve of her choice.

If you are a Calvinist, blindfold yourself and vote for random people to place it all in God's hands.

HOW TO PARTICIPATE IN ELECTIONS

Host a MAGA tailgate party outside the polling station.

If you are made to wait in line for any length of time, scream "VOTER SUPPRESSION!" at the top of your lungs.

Take the time to listen to a woman of color and ask how she would vote—like Candace Owens.

Don't let the post office deliver your ballot. Instead, hand-deliver your ballot directly to President Trump.

Bring a basin of water so you can wash your hands after voting, like Pontius Pilate.

HOW TO PARTICIPATE IN ELECTIONS

Pray. Or don't, whatever, it's cool. You do you!

Great. Now you have the basics of what it looks like to vote and participate in our fair and free elections.

But there's still so much more to cover. In the rest of this sacred book, you'll learn all about how the U.S. government works, how you get to participate in the system, and **why it all matters.**

So let's get going!

Chapter 1
The Origin Story of
American Democracy

YAY, NEW FRIENDS!

I have a bad feeling about this...

In the beginning, there was only chaos and despair. Then, man invented **DEMOCRACY**, and the world became a beautiful cornucopia of perfect joy and prosperity. To understand this flawless system and how to protect it, you must first understand where it came from. We put all our researchers to work studying the proud history of American democracy, and after scrolling through Wikipedia and watching YouTube for a few minutes, they compiled a detailed timeline more comprehensive than anything you'll get from some lame political science classes in college.

So read, learn, and educate your friends!

DEMOCRACY: HUMBLE ORIGINS

Most scientists now believe the very first democracy was created thirty-two million years ago by a group of seven single-celled gray organisms floating in a toxic primordial soup off the coast of modern-day Africa. How do scientists know this? Because they're scientists—duh. Why are you asking questions? Do you have a science degree? Sit down and listen.

Anyway, scientists tell us that the seven gray single-celled critters happened upon a small group of three orange single-celled creatures. After a quick 7-3 vote, the seven gray creatures surrounded and ate up the three orange creatures. Brutal! Democracy—rule by the majority—was born.

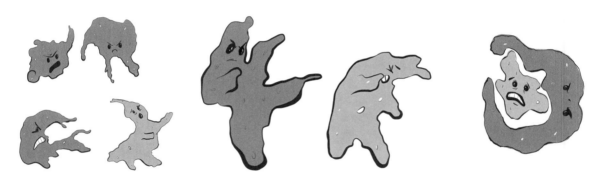

Democracy can be quite cruel—especially when the will of the majority is used to surround and destroy the minority. Over the years, the system would be improved in many ways before achieving its glorious final form in America.

ATTEMPTS AT DEMOCRACY THROUGH THE YEARS

THE GALACTIC REPUBLIC

The first known democracy existed billions of years ago in a galaxy far away, created when a galactic republic joined with a powerful order of space wizards carrying laser sticks to preserve peace and justice for all. Unfortunately, it all fell apart when a whiny sand-hating brat named Ani destroyed the republic and helped build an evil empire in its place. Sad!

ANCIENT GREECE

In 507 BC, a group of gay Greek guys called Athenians got together and came up with the first proper Earth-based democracy. Under this system, only men could vote (to be fair, this was not for patriarchal reasons, but for gay reasons), and politicians were limited to one-year terms. (Brilliant!) Unfortunately, a general named Pericles rose to power and decided all that democracy stuff was pretty gay, so Greece began to be ruled by strong aristocrats.

THE ROMAN EMPIRE

As in Greece, Rome also had a representative democracy in which only the family patriarchs could be involved in the political process. It worked pretty well until all the politicians became corrupt pedophiles (which would never happen here in America) and a powerful caesar named Augustus decided all this democracy stuff was for the birds. Rome soon came under the rule of strong aristocrats. We're sensing a theme here!

MAGNA CARTA

After many years of forgetting about all that "democracy" stuff, King John ascended to the throne of England, and he was literally the worst. Everyone hated him. Since everyone was sick and tired of King John being so awful all the time, one guy raised his hand and said, "Hey! Maybe we should try this democracy thing again!" So they all got together and drafted the Magna Carta, which limited the bad stuff a king could do. Neat!

Twas the Magna of times, Twas the Outer of times

MAYFLOWER COMPACT

When the Pilgrims set sail for the New World, they had to cram themselves into a small ship with a bunch of strangers, which led to all sorts of temptation. Everyone started bickering and fighting like toddlers in the back seat of a minivan, so they drafted a document setting the terms of self-governance in the New World.

All these lame attempts at democracy didn't quite do the trick.

THE AMERICAN REVOLUTION: A NEW DAWN . . . FOR DEMOCRACY

In the year 1776, the land was ruled by the forces of darkness and a British madman named King George III who forced everyone to drink tea instead of coffee and drive on the wrong side of the road. Horrible! They also ran an international slave-trading ring to provide labor for their evil empire. Yikes!

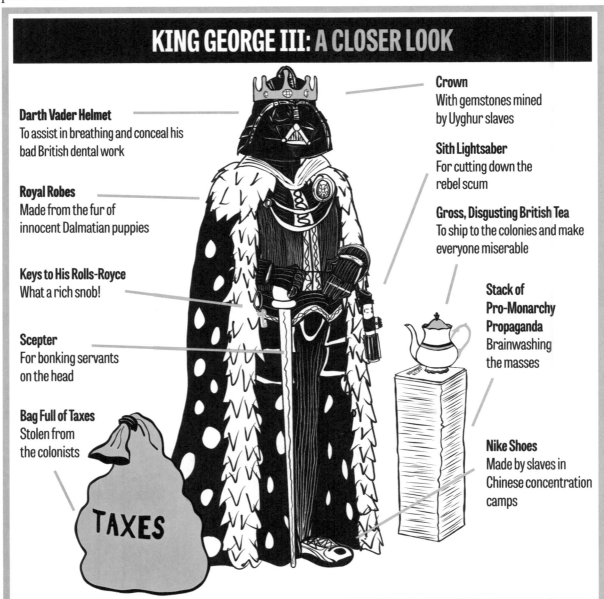

KING GEORGE III: A CLOSER LOOK

Crown
With gemstones mined by Uyghur slaves

Darth Vader Helmet
To assist in breathing and conceal his bad British dental work

Sith Lightsaber
For cutting down the rebel scum

Royal Robes
Made from the fur of innocent Dalmatian puppies

Gross, Disgusting British Tea
To ship to the colonies and make everyone miserable

Keys to His Rolls-Royce
What a rich snob!

Stack of Pro-Monarchy Propaganda
Brainwashing the masses

Scepter
For bonking servants on the head

Bag Full of Taxes
Stolen from the colonists

Nike Shoes
Made by slaves in Chinese concentration camps

TAXES

The British Empire was spreading all across the world, bringing death, slavery, and Shakespeare everywhere it went.

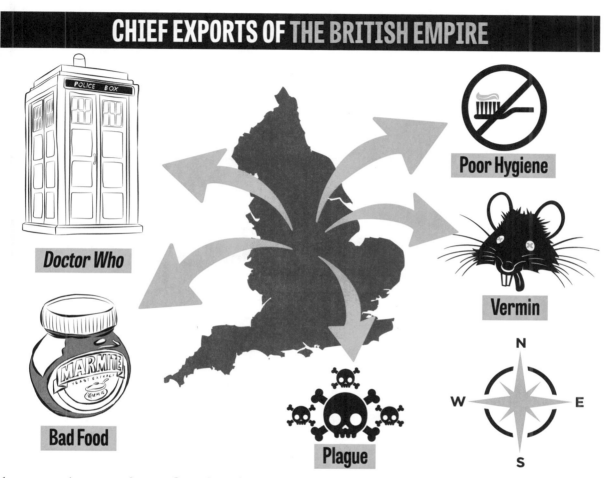

CHIEF EXPORTS OF THE BRITISH EMPIRE

Doctor Who

Bad Food

Poor Hygiene

Vermin

Plague

Americans began to form a **fiercely independent spirit,** which is usually what happens when you allow people on the other side of the ocean to practice the Protestant form of Christianity too long. Many Americans began to think: "Hey, why do we even need these British rulers, anyway?" and "Why are we paying taxes to fund King George's Sunday afternoon carriage rides?" and "Why are there a bunch of smelly British soldiers living in my home?"

The British were also sending shipments of things the colonists didn't want, like tea, beans on toast, and slaves. Yes, that's right: At this time, groups of crazy Protestants like Puritans and Quakers had become such a part of American culture that everyone started to feel really bad about slavery. Several colonies tried to outlaw the slave trade, but King George overruled those laws and sent them slaves anyway. **How rude**!

As resentment grew among the colonists against British rule, King George tried to assert his authority even more strongly by sending more soldiers to occupy colonial cities. He would not let the freedom-loving colonists have their way. All hope seemed lost, until **a very wonderful thing happened**:

A child named Kirin-El was sent to Earth from a doomed planet in another galaxy. His space pod crash-landed in a small town in Virginia, where it was discovered by a kindly Christian couple named Mary and Augustine Washington.

They took the extraterrestrial child home and raised him as their own.

THEY NAMED HIM GEORGE.

When George Washington came of age, he had been instilled with such a love of American butt-kicking freedom that he decided it was time to get a team together to fight against the British. He then started a blog and YouTube channel to radicalize the colonial youth to love freedom. Once he had an army of freedom fighters, it was time to inform King George they would no longer be needing his services through a document called **the Declaration of Independence.**

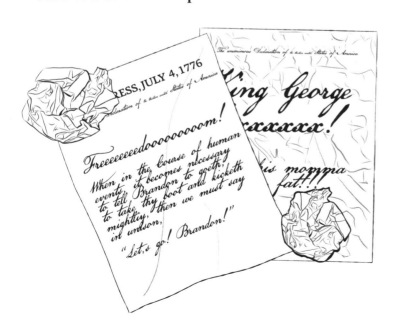

Legend says George Washington wrote the first draft of the Declaration of Independence. The first draft needed some work.

After some translation and wordsmithing from his friend Thomas Jefferson, we ended up with our famous Declaration of Independence as we know it today:

THE DECLARATION

OF INDEPENDENCE

George Washington and his pals then mailed the Declaration to King George,

AND THE REVOLUTIONARY
WAR FOR INDEPENDENCE BEGAN.

WEAPONS USED IN THE REVOLUTIONARY WAR

- MUSKETS
- CANNONS
- BRUTAL INSULTS
- PASSIVE-AGGRESSIVE COMMENTS ABOUT YOUR MOTHER-IN-LAW
- BRITISH HYGIENE
- POINTED STICKS
- FRESH FRUIT
- MIND-CONTROLLED ATTACK MOOSE

THE COMPLETELY TRUE STORY OF THE REVOLUTIONARY WAR

When the War for Independence began, General Washington was limited to just three hundred Spartans and a handful of X-wing fighters. In order to have enough power to fight the evil British Empire, he first had to travel to each of the thirteen colonies and acquire the shattered pieces of an ancient relic—a golden snake with mysterious, otherworldly powers. Only when the sacred relics were combined would he have the power of DEMOCRACY to defeat the evil forces of darkness that preyed upon the land.

JOIN, or DIE.

After venturing through the mountains, plains, and swamps of the thirteen colonies, Washington finally collected all the pieces, uniting the colonies and gaining the ancient powers of democracy to fight British tyranny. We celebrate this pivotal moment with today's "DON'T TREAD ON ME" flag.

Next, Washington needed an army. He strategically radicalized colonial youth using dank memes on Reddit and 4chan until he had enough crazy-eyed fighters to face down King George's stormtroopers.

TIMELINE OF THE

START

1770 – BOSTON MASSACRE
The British murdered fifty million people in Boston. Not even the younglings survived.

AND NOT JUST THE MEN...

1773 – BOSTON TEA PARTY
Americans culturally appropriated Native dress, protested taxes, and insurrected a British ship to dump their gross tea in the harbor. Many consider this to be the most right-wing day in American history.

1777 – AMERICAN FORCES WIN KEY BATTLE
after holding off an army of British Orcs at Helms Deep. They also win battles at Saratoga, which is pretty cool, too.

CAN YOU HEAR ME NOW?

1777–1778 – ALL SEEMS LOST
American soldiers have no shoes and DoorDash doesn't deliver to where they are stationed in Valley Forge. Also, no WiFi. Sad!

CROISSANT!

OUI, OUI!

LES INCOMPETENTS

1778 – FRENCH REINFORCEMENTS ARRIVE
With a fleet of brand new X-wings and Ornithopters. Sweet!

REVOLUTIONARY WAR

LISTEN UP, BUCKO!

1775

1775 – WASHINGTON NAMED [COM]MANDER OF CONTINENTAL ARMY
...hen begins radicalizing the youth to fight for ...om using memes and Jordan Peterson videos.

1776 – CROSSING OF THE DELAWARE RIVER
Washington and his Spec Ops team conduct a sneak attack on the British during Christmas. The crossing takes a long time as they have to pose in the middle of the river for the artist to finish his painting.

1776 – DECLARATION OF [IN]DEPENDENCE IS SIGNED
The first draft was called
...ew You, George, You Foppish Loon,"
...homas Jefferson wisely changed it!

AND HOLD...

GAIN ONE INDEPENDENCE

1776

... – AMERICANS CONDUCT CLIMACTIC, ...RING ATTACK ON BRITISH WHEN ALL HOPE SEEMS LOST
...George Washington destroys British stronghold ...ehandedly without even using a targeting computer.

1781

FINISH !

1781 – THE BRITISH FINALLY SURRENDER

THE FOUNDING FATHERS: A CLOSER LOOK

Now that Americans had their own country, it was time to create a system of government other than a monarchy that would preserve order while ensuring freedom in the New World. Not an easy task! Such an accomplishment would require a meeting of the most brilliant minds in the world— an elite team of political geniuses called the Founding Fathers.

1. GEORGE WASHINGTON
The most epic warrior king ever to walk the earth.

2. JOHN ADAMS
Fat guy, highly unlikable, lawyer. Not sure how this guy ended up in office.

3. JAMES MADISON
He wrote some of the Federalist Papers, but slacked a little bit and let Alexander Hamilton write most of them.

4. THOMAS JEFFERSON
Responsible for most of the liberties and protections in our Constitution, but he owned slaves so he's bad.

5. BENJAMIN FRANKLIN
Elon Musk's great-, great-, great-, great-grandfather, we think.

6. ALEXANDER HAMILTON
Always insisted on debating via dance battle, which annoyed everyone. Wrote most of the Federalist Papers.

7. PATRICK HENRY
An unhinged maniac who preferred death over not having liberty.

8. SAM ADAMS
A dangerous alt-right extremist who founded the Sons of Liberty, which was basically the Proud Boys of that time. Also brewed decent beer.

9. JOHN HANCOCK
The proud inventor of the signature, cousin to Herbie.

. . . AND ALL THESE OTHER GUYS NO ONE KNOWS ABOUT.
THEY DID SOMETHING TOO, PROBABLY.
GOOD JOB, GUYS!

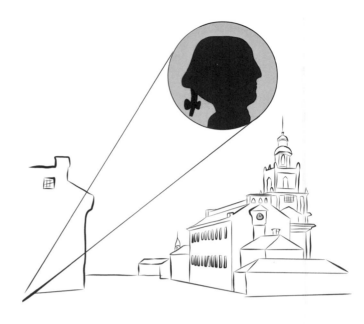

When the time was right, George Washington stood on the roof of Independence Hall and shone the Founding Father symbol into the night sky, signaling it was time to assemble.

Then, one fateful night, the Founding Fathers gathered to discuss how to govern the colonies. They acquired over seventy kegs of Samuel Adams' Boston Lager, and their wives made them delicious casseroles.

It was quite the gathering. Sparks flew. Emotions ran high.

There were even over thirteen hours of debate on whether the new country should speak English, French, or Quenya. After weeks of fierce debate and several fistfights, a little-known Founding Father named Steve raised his hand from the back of the room and said, "Hey guys, what if we try that democracy/republic thing again and see if it works this time?"

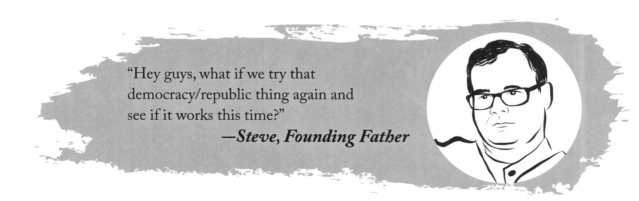

"Hey guys, what if we try that democracy/republic thing again and see if it works this time?"
—*Steve, Founding Father*

The exhausted delegates decided that was a good idea.

And so began the drafting of a document of pure genius, the climactic crowning achievement of humanity's 2,500 years of striving for freedom. After centuries of being ruled by the sword, mankind would be ruled by the pen, their consciences, and the Creator of the Universe.

The Founders created a system of power centers that would be pitted against each other, a Rube Goldberg machine of complex, interacting systems designed to prevent the government from growing too powerful and tyrannical.

The Founders completed their work by writing the single greatest political documents ever written: the U.S. Constitution and the Bill of Rights. Their work was immortalized forever, and would bring hope and liberty to millions around the world. They then drew a cool invisible map on the back leading to their buried treasure.

Not a bad start for America! Over time, the citizens would grow into the Founders' ideals, extending freedom and justice to more and more people.

But given enough time, corruption, and stupidity, humans are capable of messing up just about anything.

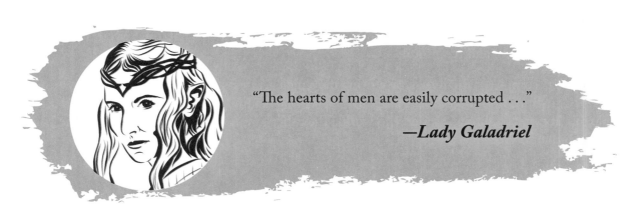

"The hearts of men are easily corrupted . . ."

—*Lady Galadriel*

CHAPTER REVIEW: THE ORIGIN STORY OF AMERICAN DEMOCRACY

We've discussed so many incredible things in these last few pages. Let's take a minute to check our comprehension for absolutely no reason whatsoever.

1. Who would win: The most powerful empire in the world, or one wooden-teeth boy?

2. What's the Revolutionary War going on in your life right now? Give it to God.

3. Show your love for your country by singing "The Star-Spangled Banner" right this second.

4. The rallying cry of the Revolution was "No Taxation Without Representation," but Murray Rothbard once wrote, "the State is a gang of thieves writ large"—perhaps echoing Augustine, who once said, "Kingdoms without justice are mere robberies." Please explain in the space provided below how electing representatives who impose taxes upon others sidesteps this and justifies the American Revolution.

5. Is Jesus Christ the Founding Father in your life? Why not?

6. Will you, right now, declare independence from Satan's fetters?

Chapter 2

Choosing Your
Political Party

Our culture talks a lot about identity these days. Whether you're a Christian or an atheist, a man or a woman, a metalhead or a goth, identity is important.

But there's perhaps nothing so important in your identity as your political party. It's the most significant thing about you. Your political party helps codify and define your beliefs around important issues. But most importantly, it helps you know who the good guys are (those in your political party) and who the bad guys are (those in the other political party).

Let's take a look at all the options available:

A COMPREHENSIVE GUIDE TO ALL OF THE POLITICAL PARTIES

DEMOCRATS

THE PARTY OF BIG GOVERNMENT
AND FREE STUFF

REPUBLICANS

THE PARTY OF SLIGHTLY LESS
GOVERNMENT AND SLIGHTLY
LESS FREE STUFF

LIBERTARIANS

THE PARTY OF DRUGS, GUNS, AND
BEER. YEEHAW!

GREEN PARTY

THE PARTY OF *FERNGULLY*
AND COMMUNISM

WHIGS

THIS FUN PARTY HAS REALLY
COOL POWDERED WIGS

TORIES

ENTIRELY MADE UP OF PEOPLE
NAMED TORY. MEETINGS HAVE
GOOD CASSEROLES.

THE TEA PARTY

OPPOSES TAXES AND HAS TOTALLY
AWESOME TRI-CORNERED HATS.
MIGHT THROW YOU IN BOSTON
HARBOR IF YOU'RE NOT CAREFUL.

BIRTHDAY PARTY

KANYE WEST'S PARTY:
WHERE EVERYONE GETS FREE
BIRTHDAY CAKE.

POOL PARTY

FORGET POLITICS. CANNONBALL!

ANARCHIST NON-PARTY PARTY

THIS PARTY IS TOTALLY NOT A
POLITICAL PARTY.
DOWN WITH THE GOVERNMENT!

**SOCIETY FOR THE PROMOTION OF
ELFISH WELFARE**

A PARTY FOR THE DISMANTLING OF
OPPRESSIVE SYSTEMS OF POWER
KEEPING HOUSE ELVES ENSLAVED.
DOBBY IS FREEEEEEEEEEE!!!!!

NEVER-NUDE PARTY

THERE ARE DOZENS OF THEM.
DOZENS!

**DEMOCRATIC SOCIALISTS
OF AMERICA**

LESS OF A PARTY AND MORE OF A
GIANT PRACTICAL JOKE.
HILARIOUS SATIRE OF THE LEFT

TRUMP

NEEDS NO EXPLANATION.
IT'S JUST DONALD TRUMP.

THE KODOS PARTY

DON'T BLAME ME. I VOTED FOR
KODOS!

THE TWO-PARTY SYSTEM

Wow, that's a lot to choose from!

Luckily, we have a two-party system. How does that work? Well, you can join any of the above political parties, but only two of them have an actual chance of getting elected: Democrats and Republicans. And maaaaaybe Libertarians, but that's pretty rare, since they always shoot themselves in the foot by having nude people run around at their conventions or do mushrooms during speeches.

Since only two political parties really have any kind of chance of getting elected, the remainder of the chapter will deal solely with the Democratic Party and Republican Party . . . and the Libertarian Party just for lulz.

Let's take a look at the viable political parties' positions on various important issues to help you get a clearer idea of where they stand:

COMPARISON OF POLICY POSITIONS

 **TAXES**

DEMOCRATS	REPUBLICANS	LIBERTARIANS
PRO	ANTI	TRIGGEEERRRRRED!!!!!!

DONUTS

DEMOCRATS	REPUBLICANS	LIBERTARIANS
Free donuts for everyone, distributed based on race and level of oppression.	Slightly fewer free donuts for everyone, distributed based on your loyalty to President Trump.	This is my donut. Come and take it!

 **WAR**

DEMOCRATS	REPUBLICANS	LIBERTARIANS
PRO	PRO	Anti-war, the goshdarn hippies! Why do they hate America so much?

CLIMATE CHANGE

DEMOCRATS	REPUBLICANS	LIBERTARIANS
Climate change is the end of human civilization as we know it and there's nothing we can do about it, but you still need to pay way more taxes to try to stop it. RUN FOR YOUR LIVES!!!	Climate change is a hoax perpetrated by Al Gore and George Soros and maybe space lizards. Besides, them folks up in Minnesota could use some climate change, eh? EH?!	Climate change is fine as long as it's private companies and not the government causing it.

COMPARISON OF POLICY POSITIONS (CONTINUED)

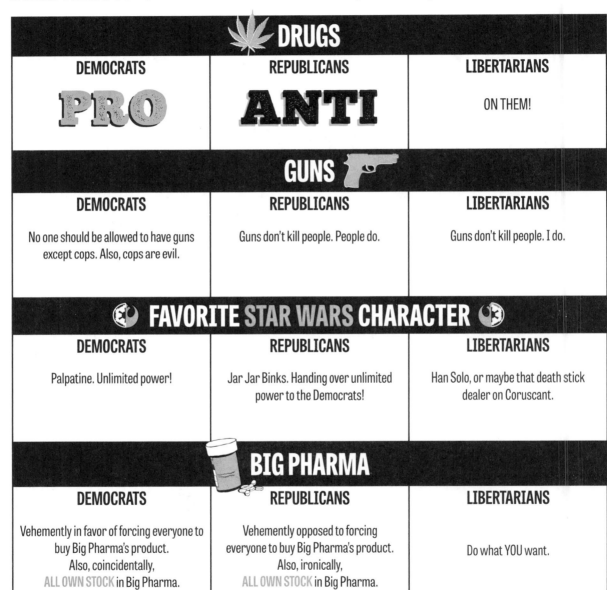

🌿 DRUGS

DEMOCRATS	REPUBLICANS	LIBERTARIANS
PRO	ANTI	ON THEM!

GUNS 🔫

DEMOCRATS	REPUBLICANS	LIBERTARIANS
No one should be allowed to have guns except cops. Also, cops are evil.	Guns don't kill people. People do.	Guns don't kill people. I do.

🌑 FAVORITE STAR WARS CHARACTER 🌑

DEMOCRATS	REPUBLICANS	LIBERTARIANS
Palpatine. Unlimited power!	Jar Jar Binks. Handing over unlimited power to the Democrats!	Han Solo, or maybe that death stick dealer on Coruscant.

BIG PHARMA

DEMOCRATS	REPUBLICANS	LIBERTARIANS
Vehemently in favor of forcing everyone to buy Big Pharma's product. Also, coincidentally, ALL OWN STOCK in Big Pharma.	Vehemently opposed to forcing everyone to buy Big Pharma's product. Also, ironically, ALL OWN STOCK in Big Pharma.	Do what YOU want.

COMPARISON OF POLICY POSITIONS (CONTINUED)

PUPPIES

DEMOCRATS	REPUBLICANS	LIBERTARIANS
They hate them, according to Republicans.	They hate them, according to Democrats.	You have the right to own a high-capacity assault puppy.

BABIES

DEMOCRATS	REPUBLICANS	LIBERTARIANS
ANTI	PRO	It's complicated.

OIL

DEMOCRATS	REPUBLICANS	LIBERTARIANS
All for oil as long as it's being used to power their electric cars and build solar panels.	YEEHAW! DRILL, BABY, DRILL!	Fossil fuels are good because they power my massive Bitcoin mining rig.

COUNTRY MUSIC

DEMOCRATS	REPUBLICANS	LIBERTARIANS
There's not enough indigenous trans representation in country music.	Country music ain't what it used to be.	Hehe. Wait—what, bro? What are we talking about? Can, like, one of you pass me another brownie? Brooooo. The colors, man. The colors!

That sums up pretty much all the important issues. Hopefully this has helped explain the different political parties' viewpoints on important issues.

Also, now we're hungry for donuts and want to watch *Star Wars*.

THE POLITICAL COMPASS

One fun way to think about politics is in terms of the political compass.

This handy graphic representation of beliefs helps us quantify where we might sit on an axis from libertarian to authoritarian and from left to right.

Here are some famous people and where they sit on the chart:

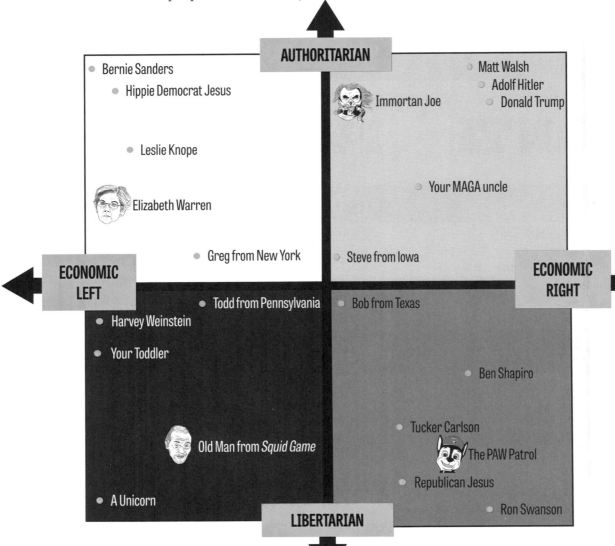

Where do you sit on the chart?
Color yourself right in there with a crayon.

HOW TO SPOT THE DIFFERENT POLITICAL PARTIES

Use this handy field guide to help yourself identify members of the different political parties when you're out and about:

HOW TO SPOT A REPUBLICAN

ALWAYS white and male, regardless of race or gender

MAGA Hat
Signed by Trump

Dead Eyes
Clearly communicate they want to control women's bodies

Smug Look of Superiority
Republicans are better than you and they know it

Dole-Kemp '96 T-shirt
They still haven't gotten over it

Leftist Tears Tumbler
Drink 'em in

Well-Worn MyPillow
Soaked with the tears of the 2020 election night

Manspreading
To assert dominance over others

Fully Semi-Automatic Ghost Gun
Weighs as much as ten boxes

Bible
(ornamental only, never read)

HOW TO SPOT A DEMOCRAT

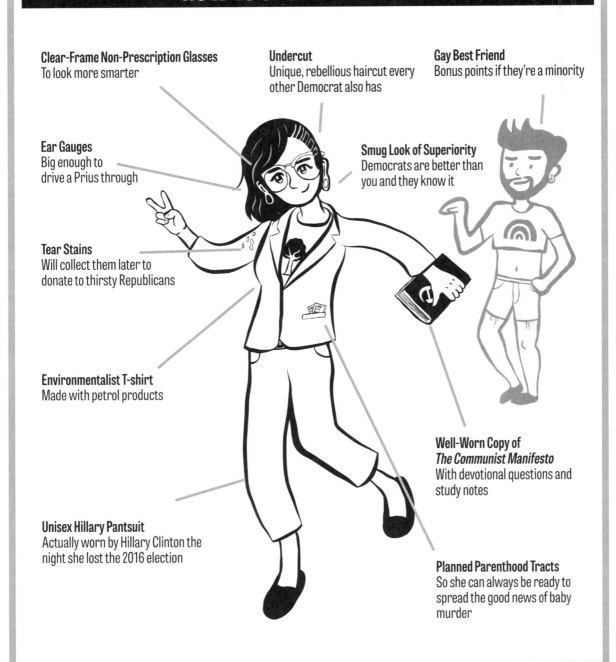

Clear-Frame Non-Prescription Glasses
To look more smarter

Undercut
Unique, rebellious haircut every other Democrat also has

Gay Best Friend
Bonus points if they're a minority

Ear Gauges
Big enough to drive a Prius through

Smug Look of Superiority
Democrats are better than you and they know it

Tear Stains
Will collect them later to donate to thirsty Republicans

Environmentalist T-shirt
Made with petrol products

Well-Worn Copy of
The Communist Manifesto
With devotional questions and study notes

Unisex Hillary Pantsuit
Actually worn by Hillary Clinton the night she lost the 2016 election

Planned Parenthood Tracts
So she can always be ready to spread the good news of baby murder

HOW TO SPOT A LIBERTARIAN

Suspicious-Smelling Cigarette
He's carrying it "for a friend"

Nonexistent Girlfriend
The fedora hasn't yet
worked its magic

Gadsden Flag Shirt
Purchased with stimulus check

Attractive Fedora
Guaranteed to work its
magic on the females

Listening to His Own Podcast
His mom is the other listener

Ron Paul Neck Tattoo
Ron Paul 4 lyfe <3

Smug Look of Superiority
Libertarians are better than
you and they know it

**Carries Boring-Sounding
Books Around**
So many pages! UGH.

Definitely Skips Leg Day
Legs smaller than his respect
for the federal government

SO, WHICH PARTY SHOULD I JOIN?

After all that info, where do you fit in? Check this handy flowchart to figure it out:

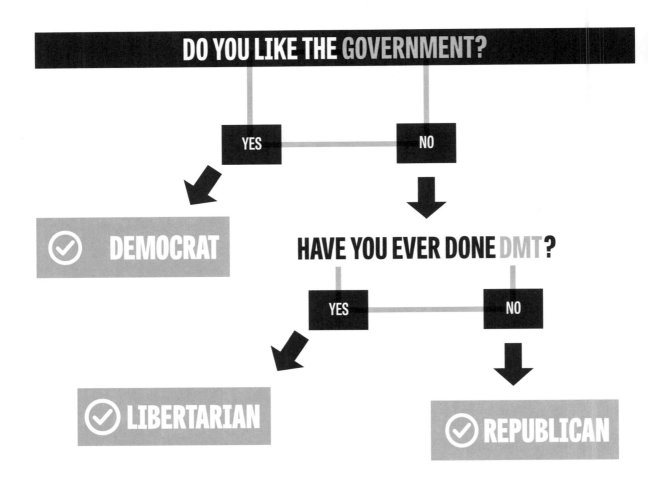

Now that you've picked your political party, it's time to get some good old-fashioned knowledge. Read on to find out how the American political system works and how you can spend every waking moment working to ensure your political party wins the day!

CHAPTER REVIEW: CHOOSING YOUR POLITICAL PARTY

We've discussed so many incredible things in these last few pages. Let's take a minute to check our comprehension for absolutely no reason whatsoever.

1. Have you ever voted Libertarian? LULZ why would you do such a thing?

2. Make up your own political party and list its 117 core platform positions below.

3. Have you ever done DMT? Describe the experience.

4. George Washington once said that "political parties may now and then answer popular ends," but "they are likely in the course of time and things, to become potent engines, by which cunning, ambitious, and unprincipled men will be enabled to subvert the power of the people and to usurp for themselves the reins of government, destroying afterwards the very engines which have lifted them to unjust dominion." But since these institutions have come down to us through the wisdom of our ancestors (what G. K. Chesterton would call the "democracy of the dead"), what would be your political party's platform? Be specific as to how your party would usurp for itself the reins of government to accomplish your very good intentions.

5. Which political party has your favorite colors?

Chapter 3

The
Legislative Branch

Now it's time to take a look at our modern-day political system. To start with, let's learn about the branches of government, starting with the legislative branch.

Laws are what separate us from the animals. Without laws, we'd just be a bunch of monkeys throwing feces at each other.

We are civilized.   We have order.

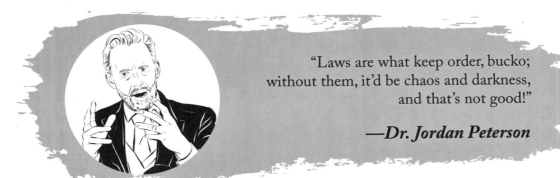

"Laws are what keep order, bucko; without them, it'd be chaos and darkness, and that's not good!"

—*Dr. Jordan Peterson*

But **somebody** has to make the laws. And that's the job of the legislative branch.

Let's take a look at how it works:

THE LEGISLATIVE BRANCH: MAKIN' DA LAW

SENATE

- Made up of two senators from each state regardless of size, so finally Montana can feel important.
- The vice president breaks ties. So she can finally feel important.
- Approves president's nominees to SCOTUS, which usually involves lots of reasoned debate and calm, rational discussion.
- Can impeach the president, which is always done only for the most egregious of infractions, like phone calls to Ukraine.
- Senators serve six-year terms, though all of them are over 127 years old.

HOUSE OF REPRESENTATIVES

- Representation is based on size of state, so California and New York decide basically everything.
- The vice president is completely meaningless here. Not even allowed to use the restrooms.
- The House originates the spending bills, so lobbyists prefer to hang out with these folks.
- Known as the "lower chamber" of Congress, which means they don't have to wear top hats and monocles.
- Representatives serve two years, though all of them are over 127 years old except MTG and AOC.

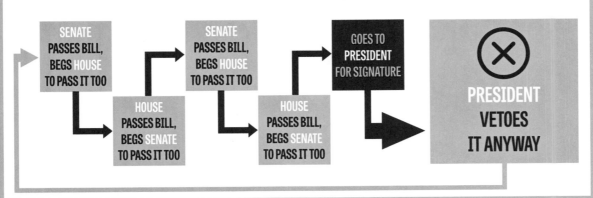

EVOLUTION OF A LEGISLATOR

On Election Day, citizens of each state choose representatives and senators to be their voice in the halls of government, make just and useful laws, and protect them from overreach. None of that happens, of course, but that's the idea. In the last few centuries, Washington, D.C., has been overtaken by an unseen evil Cthulhu from the Great Beyond that corrupts the minds, hearts and intentions of everyone who goes there. Over time, the politician will become assimilated into a self-propagating, Borg-like abomination that consumes all in its path. Not good! Here's how the process works:

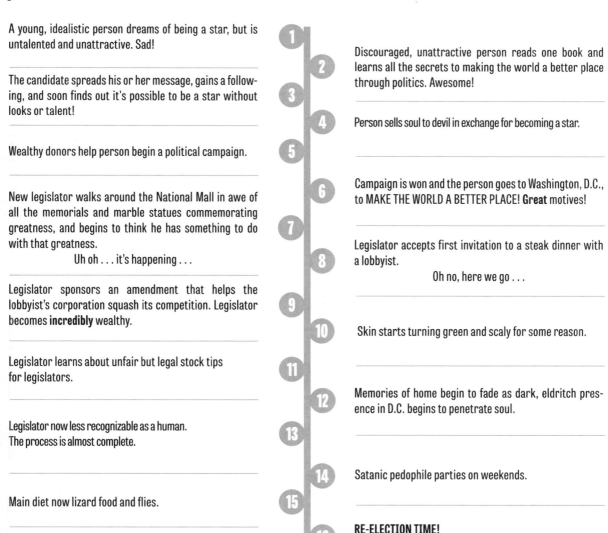

1. A young, idealistic person dreams of being a star, but is untalented and unattractive. Sad!

2. Discouraged, unattractive person reads one book and learns all the secrets to making the world a better place through politics. Awesome!

3. The candidate spreads his or her message, gains a following, and soon finds out it's possible to be a star without looks or talent!

4. Person sells soul to devil in exchange for becoming a star.

5. Wealthy donors help person begin a political campaign.

6. Campaign is won and the person goes to Washington, D.C., to MAKE THE WORLD A BETTER PLACE! **Great** motives!

7. New legislator walks around the National Mall in awe of all the memorials and marble statues commemorating greatness, and begins to think he has something to do with that greatness.
Uh oh . . . it's happening . . .

8. Legislator accepts first invitation to a steak dinner with a lobbyist.
Oh no, here we go . . .

9. Legislator sponsors an amendment that helps the lobbyist's corporation squash its competition. Legislator becomes **incredibly** wealthy.

10. Skin starts turning green and scaly for some reason.

11. Legislator learns about unfair but legal stock tips for legislators.

12. Memories of home begin to fade as dark, eldritch presence in D.C. begins to penetrate soul.

13. Legislator now less recognizable as a human. The process is almost complete.

14. Satanic pedophile parties on weekends.

15. Main diet now lizard food and flies.

16. RE-ELECTION TIME!
(At least he's not as bad as the other guy!)

FAMOUS LEGISLATORS THROUGH HISTORY

The United States is a representative democracy, meaning we don't pass laws directly. That would lead to all of us collectively voting for dumb stuff.

This is known as "mob rule" and it's not good, bucko. So, instead of voting in dumb laws ourselves, we vote for representatives who vote in dumb laws on our behalf. These are called legislators. On the federal level, they're made up of senators and representatives. They're always upstanding people of the highest moral character.

Here are some of the most famous senators and congresspeople throughout history:

1. **NANCY PELOSI**—Insider trading / fridge / $12 ice cream / eyebrows

2. **JAMES WILLIAM GAZLAY**—Edited a weekly paper called the *Western Tiller*, according to Wikipedia. Hey, they can't all be superstars.

3. **JAR JAR BINKS**—Moved to grant emergency powers to the Chancellor during the Clone Wars. Might have been a secret Sith Lord.

4. **ILHAN OMAR**—A family woman if ever there was one.

5. **TED CRUZ**—Let's be honest. He was only elected for his raw masculinity and rugged good looks.

6. **AOC**—Fantastic dancer. Great drink maker. Mortal enemy of garbage disposal.

7. **TED KENNEDY**—The Lion of the Senate—an inspiring and stalwart example of righteous senatorial tenacity. Never killed a woman by driving her into a lake.

8. **RON PAUL**—The only legislator backed by the gold standard, and Russia.

9. **FRANK UNDERWOOD**—Keep him away from your kids.

10. **JOHN C. CALHOUN**—Really, really liked slavery, for some reason. Cool hair though.

11. **MTG**—Like AOC, but for the right. Dance moves not as good.

12. **STEVE SCALISE**—Bulletproof.

13. **RASHI . . . RASHIDA TL . . . TLAI . . .** Never mind.

14. **DAN CRENSHAW**—Has a cool eyepatch.

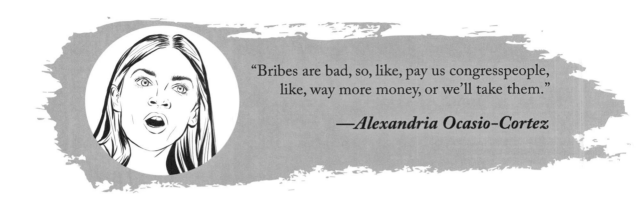

"Bribes are bad, so, like, pay us congresspeople, like, way more money, or we'll take them."

—*Alexandria Ocasio-Cortez*

HOW TO BRIBE A POLITICIAN

These representatives are supposed to represent the interests of the people in their districts, also known as their constituents. How quaint!

The great thing is you can get them to do anything you want if you give them enough money. This is known as bribery and/or totally legitimate "lobbying."

Politicians gather together in something called a "cocktail party," which is like a Costco for political bribery. The men wear their finest girdles and the women wear their most expensive "tax the rich" dresses, and then they take their places on the store shelves so lobbyists can shop for the right legislators.

THE LOBBYISTS

Lobbyists have several effective currencies at their disposal, including money, power, influence, and trafficked underage sex workers from Ukraine. In return, politicians can offer unfair business advantages, corrupt new laws designed to help the lobbyist and the special interest he represents, and even cover up heinous crimes.

THE SECRET ROOM

These special events are held at top-secret underground event halls designed only for the elites. Sometimes, when those halls are all booked, they meet at the Applebee's off of Richmond Highway south of D.C.

If you are disgusted by this system, how DARE you. This is democracy. Do you really want to oppose democracy? Do you know who else opposed democracy? HITLER. Yeah, that's right.

It is true, however, that this system could use some reform. What system can't be improved, right? Well, good news! This system was recently reformed in a very meaningful way!

Now, thanks to new technology, legislators can wear special barcodes at these parties, allowing lobbyists to self-scan and check out their preferred bribed congressperson.

Much better!

DID YOU KNOW?

For the sake of convenience, most congresspeople have barcodes on their foreheads so that lobbyists can just scan them at self-checkout.

HOW A BILL BECOMES A LAW

How does a bill become a law, anyway? It's a beautiful, natural metamorphosis. The wriggling, pathetic little bill climbs out of its cocoon to become a majestic butterfly—a butterfly that sends people to jail or taxes them up the wazoo.

Now, through modern science and technology, we can finally put this beautiful process under a microscope.

Let's take a look at the step-by-step process of a bill becoming a law:

Legislator has an idea.	Legislator proposes bill in committee.
Legislators all wake up with terrible hangover..	Committee debates bill in important, late-night meeting at Hooters. It passes! Hooray! Now bring on the wings!
Bill is brought to the House or Senate floor for a vote.	Some old guy filibusters the vote. Everyone waits until he dies of old age.
Now, repeat most of these steps in the other house of Congress. The bill passes. Hooray!	Finally, a vote is held. The bill passes! Hooray!
The president signs the law IF he woke up on the right side of the bed this morning, or he vetoes it and tells Congress to get REKT.	Congress can then override the president if they have like a billion votes.

HOORAY! IT'S A LAW

DID YOU KNOW?

The longest filibuster ever was in the spring of 1850, when Senator Henry Clay performed the complete works of William Shakespeare while tap dancing to protest a bill deregulating cryptocurrency.

COMMITTEES

There's like a billion committees in Congress. No way we can list them all.

We're on a book deadline here.

But here are the most important ones:

THE MOST IMPORTANT COMMITTEES EVER

- Ways and Means Committee
- Judiciary Committee
- Dank Memes Committee
- Voting Raises for Ourselves Committee
- Be Your Own Boss and Sell Essential Oils from Home Committee
- Shuffleboard Committee
- Budget Committee
- Over Budget Committee
- *Fight Club*
- *Star Trek* Fan Committee

Now you know literally everything there is to know about the legislative branch. It's a nice branch, lots of little twigs on it and everything. It would make a fine walking stick or a sword if you were out on a walk and are into such things. Metaphorically speaking.

ONWARD, FELLOW CITIZEN!

Let's carry on and learn about the most executive-y of the branches. Next up:

The executive branch.

But before we conclude our comprehensive overview of the legislative branch, please join us on a tour of some of the most priceless relics in the history of the United States Congress.

Follow along with the tour guide, please, and don't get lost.

Wandering around in the Capitol Building without permission can result in you getting thrown in jail indefinitely with no access to legal representation.

MUSEUM OF CONGRESS

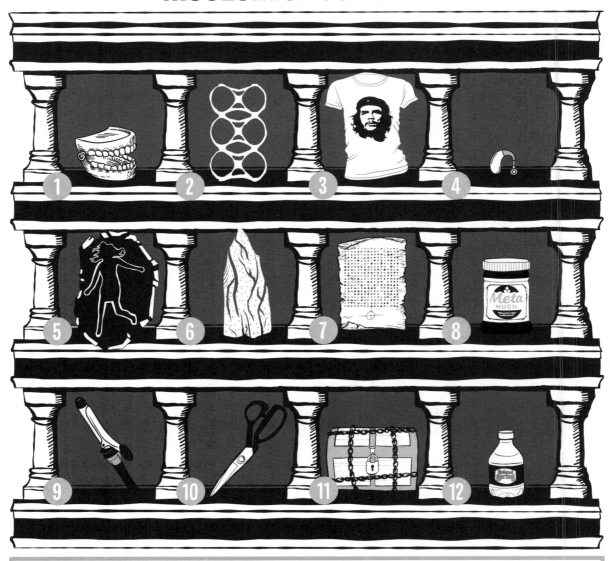

1. Nancy Pelosi's dentures
2. The plastic soda ring that was removed from poor Mitch McConnell's neck
3. Bernie Sanders's favorite Che Guevara shirt
4. Dianne Feinstein's hearing aid
5. The chalk outline where AOC died on January 6
6. The pillar of salt Newt Gingrich turned into when he looked back as he left office
7. A cryptic note with weird symbols found in Ted Cruz's office
8. Old container of Metamucil in the break room
9. Rand Paul's curling iron
10. Mitt Romney's hair-cutting scissors
11. A locked box containing Maxine Waters's sense of shame
12. Marco Rubio's water bottle

CHAPTER REVIEW: THE LEGISLATIVE BRANCH

We've discussed so many incredible things in these last few pages. Let's take a minute to check our comprehension for absolutely no reason whatsoever.

1. How much of your knowledge of the legislative branch comes from Schoolhouse Rock?

2. Ok, so in Interstellar, *Matthew McConaughey comes out of a black hole and actually influences the past, but he would've never gotten there if he hadn't influenced the past in the first place. Please explain the entire plot.*

3. Article I of the Constitution establishes the legislative branch, which is responsible for creating laws pertaining to the central government. Drawing inspiration from the eighteenth-century political philosopher Montesquieu, America has attempted to live by a separation of powers in government to ensure no one branch becomes too powerful. Do we need a fourth branch of government to make sure Congress doesn't let bureaucrats run the nation and hand over its law-writing powers to special interests and lobbyists? Please explain in the place provided below.

4. Do you remember that one time when Charles Sumner was caned by Preston Brooks? That was awesome.

5. Each of us has his own personal John C. Calhoun to face. Write yours below.

Chapter 4

The
Executive Branch

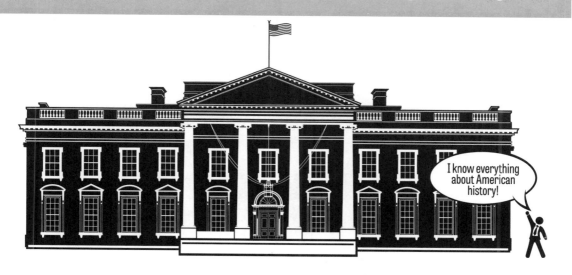

I know everything about American history!

The legislative branch may technically be the first branch of government, but the executive branch is first in our hearts. The executive branch controls so many significant things in our country: our armed forces, the execution of laws, and, of course, unilateral drone strikes on foreign countries. Kapow!

EXECUTIVE

You might even say the executive branch is the most important one of all.

While the legislative branch makes the laws (in theory anyway), and the judicial branch reviews the laws (in theory anyway), the executive branch *enforces* the laws.

(In theory, anyway.)

Let's take a look at how the executive branch works. Take a look at it in all its glory:

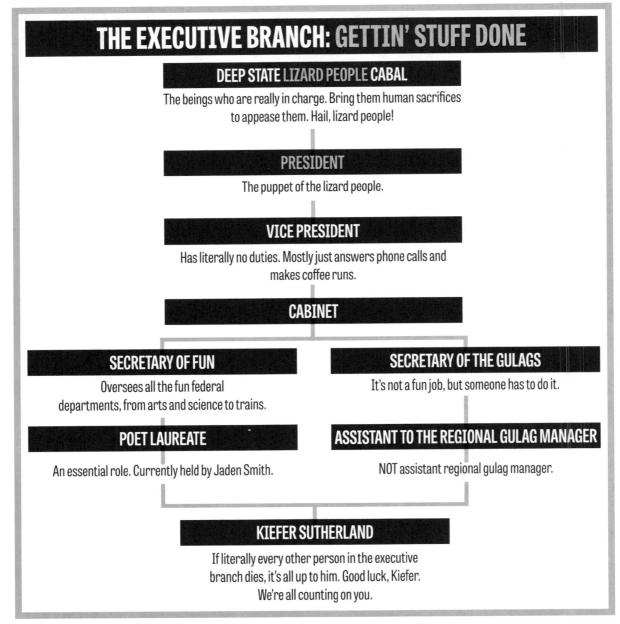

THE EXECUTIVE BRANCH: GETTIN' STUFF DONE

DEEP STATE LIZARD PEOPLE CABAL
The beings who are really in charge. Bring them human sacrifices to appease them. Hail, lizard people!

PRESIDENT
The puppet of the lizard people.

VICE PRESIDENT
Has literally no duties. Mostly just answers phone calls and makes coffee runs.

CABINET

SECRETARY OF FUN
Oversees all the fun federal departments, from arts and science to trains.

SECRETARY OF THE GULAGS
It's not a fun job, but someone has to do it.

POET LAUREATE
An essential role. Currently held by Jaden Smith.

ASSISTANT TO THE REGIONAL GULAG MANAGER
NOT assistant regional gulag manager.

KIEFER SUTHERLAND
If literally every other person in the executive branch dies, it's all up to him. Good luck, Kiefer. We're all counting on you.

THE STAR OF THE SHOW: ★ THE PRESIDENT ★

The most important figure in the federal government is the president. When we kicked King George III out and founded the country, we wanted to make sure no one man got too powerful. So, instead of a king, we decided the country would be led by a president.

Of course, the president is now way more powerful than King George III ever was, but don't worry: you get to vote for him, so it's different. Plus, he doesn't have one of those ornate golden thrones; he sits at an expensive desk in a plush room surrounded by attendants waiting on him and taking care of his every need.

So it's totally not the same.

Let's take a look at this chart for more comparisons between kings and presidents:

KING	PRESIDENT
Castle	Giant White House
Throne	Resolute Desk
Royal Decrees	Executive Orders
Royal Trumpet Boy	Press Secretary
Faithful Steed	Presidential Limo
Court Jesters	Reporters
Knights of the Round Table	SEAL Team 6

FAMOUS PRESIDENTS THROUGHOUT HISTORY

Here are some of the more well-known presidents from throughout American history. Since the public school system isn't very good, you might not have heard about some of these guys, but rest assured this is the definitive list from your trusted friends at The Babylon Bee.

George Washington

The creator of democracy and God's chosen messenger to the masses. Was excellent at ping-pong.

Andrew Jackson

Invented the $20 bill. Not a huge fan of the Indians.

Abraham Lincoln

Known primarily for his taste in hats and epic beard game. Also freed the slaves or something.

Ulysses S. Grant

Very solid beard game. Fought in the Civil War. He wasn't as virtuous as people on Twitter today, though, so if you see a statue of him you should push it over.

Teddy Roosevelt

A real man.

FDR

Not as cool as Teddy.

JFK

Killed by CIA or maybe just some crazy guy.

Bill Clinton

Played the sax and was known for his personal integrity.

Jimmy Carter

See "train wreck."

Richard Nixon

Was not a crook.

Margaret, President of Sunnyport Pines HOA in Jacksonville, FL

Not a federal president, but a real legend in Jacksonville.

George W. Bush

Master of speaking English good.

Josiah Bartlet

The perfect president.

Dwayne Elizondo Mountain Dew Camacho

Due to be elected president any day now.

David Palmer

Like a good neighbor.

President Lisa Simpson

Second president to play the sax.

Barack Obama

Read one of his seventeen memoirs.

Hillary Clinton

The **true** winner of the 2016 election. Was only defeated by Russian hackers sharing memes on Facebook. Congratulations, Madame President!

Whoever Is Telling Joe Biden What To Do

The true ruler of our country and cause of all our problems.

Donald Trump

The one true president from now until the stars fall from the sky and the universe cools into infinite heat death.
[not pictured]

BUREAUCRACY: A BEAUTIFUL THING

You might be thinking the elected officials of the executive branch are all there is to it.

Boy, are you dumb!

There are way more organizations, agencies, departments, offices, sub-offices, under-agencies, shadow organizations, sister agencies, and so on in the federal government than you can shake a stick at. The vast majority of the hundreds of thousands of officers, leaders, secretaries, and employees in these bureaucratic organizations are, of course, not elected. They are appointed in a process that is always aboveboard and never involves sleazy deals in dimly lit rooms filled with cigar smoke as briefcases of cash change hands.

That would be corrupt. Our government is many things, but it is not corrupt.

Let's take a look at some of the bureaucracies that fall under the umbrella of the federal government:

A COMPREHENSIVE LIST OF OUR BUREAUCRATIC AGENCIES

CIA The Central Intelligence Agency. Its job is to stop terrorists.

FBI The Federal Bureau of Investigation. Its job is to investigate UFOs, January 6 protesters, and parents concerned that their kids are learning critical race theory in schools.

CVS A shadowy government agency with poorly functioning self-checkout machines and ridiculously long receipts. Might be run by the CIA?

NSA The National Security Agency. Its job is also to stop terrorists.

DHS The Department of Homeland Security. Its job is also to stop terrorists.

UHF A classic Weird Al movie that was snubbed for Best Picture. Badgers? Badgers? We don't need no stinking badgers!

FFA The Future Farmers of America, also known as the kids you beat up in high school. Unless you went to high school in Iowa—then they were the kings of campus.

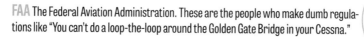

FAA The Federal Aviation Administration. These are the people who make dumb regulations like "You can't do a loop-the-loop around the Golden Gate Bridge in your Cessna."

KFC Mystical guardians of the eleven secret herbs and spices.

IRS The Internal Revenue Service, which is loosely based on the Thieves Guild from *Skyrim*. Everyone's favorite government agency.

NPS National Park Service. These guys take care of our most majestic parks, like Yellowstone, Sequoia, and Mountain View Disc Golf Park in Fresno, California.

TSA Founded in 1865 by Protestant William Booth after he witnessed a homeless man ejected from the church he attended.

WWF These guys focus on wild, muscular beasts that perform amazing feats of strength and can murder you with their raw animalistic power.

WWF These guys focus on wild, muscular beasts that perform amazing feats of strength and can murder you with their raw animalistic power.

UFC The Ultimate Fighting Championship. Associated with far-right extremist Joe Rogan. Extremely problematic.

SBG Headed by Matt Walsh, this agency is dedicated to returning shopping carts to corrals in the parking lot and promoting the extinction of pandas.

While these are all great, there is of course an unlimited number of federal bureaucracies that could possibly be created.

It's the very best thing about bureaucracies: strike one down, and two more shall take its place. Or they'll become more powerful than you can possibly imagine—whatever the reference is.

FEDERAL DEPARTMENT GENERATOR

Using this handy generator, you can create your very own federal department:

First Letter of Last Thing You Ate	First Letter of Yo Momma's Name	Third Letter of the Name of the Last Person You Texted	Ask a Friend for a Random Letter
A. Federal	A. Department	A. Oppressed	A. Potatoes
B. National	B. Ministry	B. Furtive	B. Bankruptcy
C. Official	C. Institution	C. Delicate	C. Investigations
D. Sovereign	D. Office	D. Mandalorian	D. Garbage Trucks
E. Everlasting	E. Bureau	E. Affluent	E. Eskimos
F. Supreme	F. Church	F. Homosexual	F. Homosexuals
G. International	G. Base	G. Indigenous	G. Ents
H. Dependable	H. Cabal	H. Non-White	H. Mechwarriors
I. Institutional	I. Salon	I. Undesirable	I. Choo-Choos
J. Reprehensible	J. League	J. Vestigial	J. Pollution
K. Infallible	K. Interest Group	K. Royal	K. War
L. Sacred	L. Appreciators	L. Effervescent	L. Immigrants
M. Internal	M. Mob	M. Rowdy	M. Drone Strikes
N. Fabulous	N. Queendom	N. Blessed	N. Currency
O. Homosexual	O. Dance Troupe	O. Sexy	O. Badgers
P. Cozy	P. Cottage	P. Adorable	P. Lin-Manuel Musicals
Q. All-Powerful	Q. Horde	Q. Frightening	Q. Interpretive Dance
R. Unofficial	R. Fan Club	R. Dangerous	R. Ottomans
S. Many-Colored	S. Coven	S. Flavorful	S. Breakfast
T. Immortal	T. Cult	T. Unrepentant	T. Casinos
U. Intergalactic	U. Cohort	U. Musical	U. Minorities
V. Eternal	V. Alliance	V. Homeless	V. Wizards
W. Tiny	W. Legion	W. Muscular	W. Veterans
X. Massively Multiplayer	X. Council	X. Planetary	X. Awareness
Y. Penultimate	Y. Society	Y. Extraordinary	Y. Heavy Metal
Z. Democratic	Z. Agency	Z. Lightly Toasted	Z. Doom

OF

Here are a few examples of ones we've generated:

Federal Bureau of Oppressed Potatoes

Sacred Department of Lightly Toasted Ents

Homosexual Mob of Homosexual Homosexuals

Intergalactic Coven of Sexy Badgers

Democratic Legion of Mandalorian Eskimos

All-Powerful Horde of Dangerous Ottomans

HOW EXECUTIVE ORDERS WORK

Laws can take FOREVER to pass, unless they're pay raises for Congress. Those go through pretty much immediately.

But when you need to get something done that's actually helpful, you need the president to simply pass an executive order. The great thing about executive orders is the president just shouts them out or declares them, and they get enacted.

You don't have any of that boring debate or voting that you get in Congress, so all the president's great ideas are sure to become reality.

Let's take a look at how it works:

HOW TO NAVIGATE GOVERNMENT BUREAUCRACIES

All this 100 percent accurate information about the executive branch is fine and dandy on paper.

But how does the federal government affect your everyday life? The answer is simple—EVERY area of it is touched by the government.

WHAT'S TOUCHED?

- Sidewalks
- Roads
- Haircuts
- Breathing
- Your kids' gender ideology
- Breakfast cereal
- Milk purchases
- Lemonade stands
- Spam? Probably Spam
- Gun purchases
- Nerf gun purchases (California only)
- Chemicals you're forced to inject into your body
- Price of oil
- Price of life-saving epipens
- Price of cell phone plan
- Your default web browser

With the government lovingly touching every area of your life, it must be pretty easy to deal with, right?

Wrong! You'd be surprised how hard it is to get a permit for a new chicken coop in your backyard or obtain a license to do something really dangerous, like cut someone's hair.

Hey, it's just the government keeping us safe. But, like it or not, we all have to deal with the feds at some point.

Use these simple kids' mazes to help guide you through these processes for dealing with the federal government:

HOW TO FILE YOUR TAXES

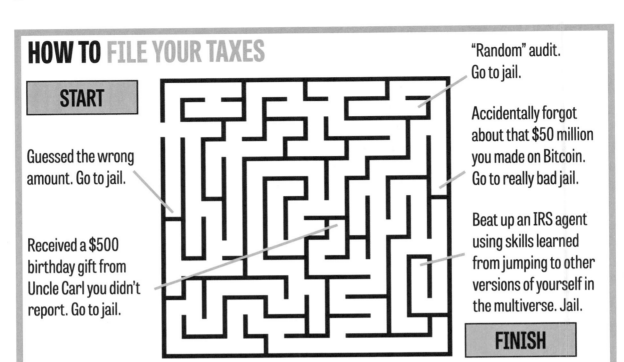

START

"Random" audit.
Go to jail.

Accidentally forgot
about that $50 million
you made on Bitcoin.
Go to really bad jail.

Guessed the wrong
amount. Go to jail.

Received a $500
birthday gift from
Uncle Carl you didn't
report. Go to jail.

Beat up an IRS agent
using skills learned
from jumping to other
versions of yourself in
the multiverse. Jail.

FINISH

HOW TO FILE FOR A BUILDING PERMIT TO ADD A DECK TO YOUR HOUSE

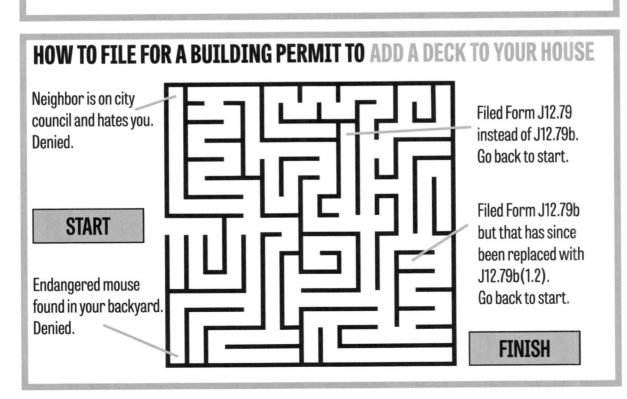

Neighbor is on city
council and hates you.
Denied.

Filed Form J12.79
instead of J12.79b.
Go back to start.

START

Filed Form J12.79b
but that has since
been replaced with
J12.79b(1.2).
Go back to start.

Endangered mouse
found in your backyard.
Denied.

FINISH

HOW TO GET A LICENSE TO RUN A BANANA STAND

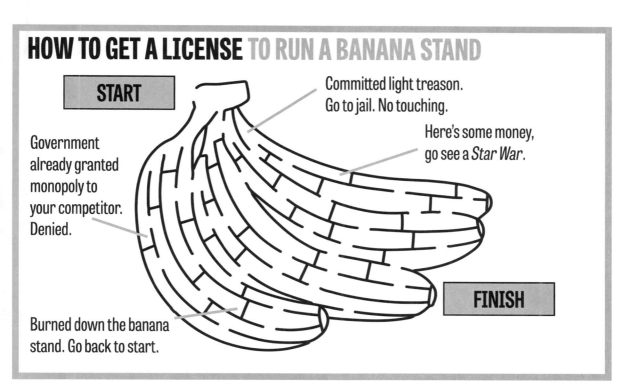

START

Committed light treason.
Go to jail. No touching.

Here's some money,
go see a *Star War*.

Government
already granted
monopoly to
your competitor.
Denied.

FINISH

Burned down the banana
stand. Go back to start.

HOW TO LEGALLY CHANGE YOUR GENDER TO A POTATO

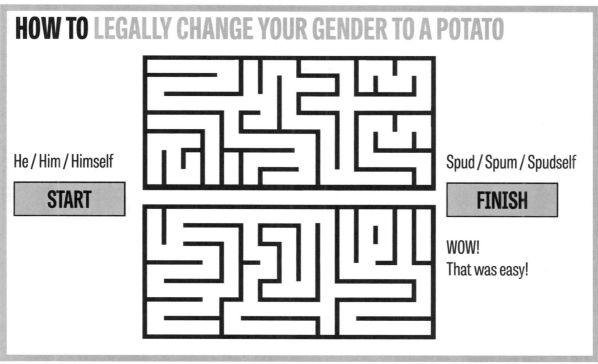

He / Him / Himself

START

Spud / Spum / Spudself

FINISH

WOW!
That was easy!

Now that you know how the executive branch works, you're one step closer to participating in our democracy! We'll take a look at some more branches of the government coming up so you'll be fully informed.

In the meantime, be sure to pray this prayer to the commander in chief each morning and evening:

O great executive officer, worthy of praise and honor,

May thou be glorified, forever and always,

May thy executive orders go forth and not return void,

May thy words be carried out to the letter as though they were a law passed by Congress,

Let thine enemies be destroyed with fire and brimstone and/or a drone strike,

And may thy pillow be cold on both sides for all thy days.

Amen!

Thanks for joining our lesson on the executive branch today.

As we exit, please take a moment to pass through our Museum of Presidents, containing all kinds of famous relics from your favorite American presidents and also Bill Clinton.

When you're done browsing, please exit through the gift shop, and do join us again soon!

MUSEUM OF PRESENTS

1. Quarter Pounder Trump left behind, naturally preserved

2. Jimmy Carter (actual size)

3. Ronald Reagan's pet eagle

4. George H. W. Bush's lips

5. The wood polish George Washington used in lieu of toothpaste

6. Trick lapel flower John Tyler used to squirt people with. Classic!

7. Copy of *Maxim* Bill Clinton kept in Oval Office drawer

8. Bucket of popcorn Lincoln was eating at Ford's Theatre

9. Document containing William Henry Harrison's detailed 32-day plan to save the country

10. George W. Bush's copy of *Hooked on Phonics*

11. Button Barack Obama used to launch drone strikes on hospitals

12. Barrel of Teddy Roosevelt's toxic masculinity

CHAPTER REVIEW: THE EXECUTIVE BRANCH

We've discussed so many incredible things in these last few pages. Let's take a minute to check our comprehension for absolutely no reason whatsoever.

1. *Why does supreme executive power derive from a mandate from the masses, not from some farcical aquatic ceremony?*

2. *List all the presidents in order of how similar they look to Dwayne "The Rock" Johnson.*

3. *Which president is on the $100 bill?*

4. *What would your first executive order be as president? Mine would be free ice cream for all. Ice cream is yummy.*

5. *President Thomas Jefferson was so concerned about going beyond his delegated powers that when confronted with attacks by Barbary pirates, he said he could "not go beyond the line of defense" and asked Congress to authorize any actions of war. In this same noble spirit, President Barack Obama once bragged, "We are not just going to be waiting for legislation . . . I've got a pen, and I've got a phone. And I can use that pen to sign executive orders." If you were president, what would be your favorite power that is found nowhere in the Constitution?.*

6. *Can you identify the bureaucracy in your life? Ask God to break those chains right now.*

Chapter 5

The
Judicial Branch

If you've been following along so far, you know that a democracy will almost never fail us. Like a mighty fortress, sure and strong, our democracy stands stalwart against the tides of anarchic chaos that would otherwise engulf us. The legislative branch passes laws that are like strong bulwarks stopping everything from descending into a warlord-ruled, post-apocalyptic hellscape like Somalia or Seattle. The executive branch enforces these laws, carrying them out perfectly and to the letter, never overreaching or accidentally oppressing its people instead of defending their rights.

BUT.

But occasionally, once in a very great while, these two branches fail us. Maybe a law isn't exactly 100 percent constitutional, or maybe the federal executive gets just a teensy bit power-hungry and decides to enslave everyone and cover all the lands with darkness.

In these very rare instances, we turn to the hallowed judicial branch to save us. While the legislators pass the laws and the executive enforces the laws, the judicial branch interprets the laws.

DID YOU KNOW?

The judicial branch was named after Judy Shellenberg, a cat lady who lived across the street from George Washington. On her rare ventures outdoors, she would chastise the children playing in the street with proclamations of, "That ain't right! Would you kids cut it out?" George was inspired by her commitment to justice, and named an entire governmental branch after her.

THE JUDICIAL BRANCH: GETTIN' JUDGEY WIT IT

GRANDE SUPREME COURT
WITH GUACAMOLE

SUPREME COURT
CAN UPGRADE TO GRANDE SUPREME W/ GUAC (FOR $3.99)

CIRCUIT COURTS
NOT TO BE CONFUSED WITH *SHORT CIRCUIT* COURTS. NEED INPUT, STEPHANIE!

LOWER-LEVEL TRIAL COURTS
THIS IS WHERE YOU GO WHEN YOU RUN A RED LIGHT OR STEAL SOMETHING FROM A MUSEUM

PEOPLE'S COURT
IT'S ON TV WHEN YOU'RE HOME SICK FROM SCHOOL

TENNIS COURTS
VERDICT: LOVE

FOOD COURT
MMM ... CINNABON

BASKETBALL COURTS
OUTSIDE OF THE SCHOOL

COURT OF OWLS
SAVE US, BATMAN!

QUART OF MILK
WE HAD TO FILL SPACE HERE, OK?

COURT OF PUBLIC OPINION
TWITTER POLL FINDS YOU GUILTY

COURTING
WHICH IS WAY BETTER THAN DATING

THE MOST NOTORIOUS JUSTICES

Of course, the heart and soul of the justice system are the judges and justices themselves. Judges are typically political appointments, while Supreme Court justices are nominated by the president himself.

They also serve for life, meaning you get a lot of Supreme Court justices who look like the zombies from *The Walking Dead*. Let's take a look at some of the more prominent ones:

1. **JUDGE DREDD**—Not just a judge, but the actual embodiment of the law itself.

2. **THE NOTORIOUS RBG**—Served on the Court for over 228 years before passing away at the young age of 722.

3. **BOOK OF JUDGES**—"Adoni-Bezek fled, but they chased him and caught him, and cut off his thumbs and big toes." Judges 1:6

4. **CHIEF JUSTICE JOHN JAY**—The first chief justice of the U.S. Supreme Court, which means he mostly ruled on disputes over cattle.

5. **VICTORIA JUSTICE**—In her victory, just remember SHE.

6. **BRETT KAVANAUGH**—Does this guy know how to party or what? Right on!

7. **CLARENCE THOMAS**—Takes a unique approach to his duties on the Supreme Court by actually attempting to interpret the law. LOL.

8. **AMY CONEY BARRETT**—Has adopted seven more kids not pictured since this went to print.

9. **JUDGE JUDY**—The most feared of all judges.

10. **JUDGE REINHOLD**—His name is Judge.

11. **MIKE JUDGE**—Yup. Yup. Yup. Mmmhmm.

12. **JESUS CHRIST, SOVEREIGN LORD AND JUDGE OF THE UNIVERSE**—In the end, the only Judge that matters.

THE MOST NOTORIOUS COURT CASES

BROWN v. BOARD OF EDUCATION OF TOPEKA

In this case, the Supreme Court ended the segragation of schools. Three people in Mississippi are still angry about this decision.

ROE v. WADE

Landmark abortion case when the court ruled that women have the right to kill their children with impunity.

Reasonable, right?

BUSH v. GORE

A historic case when the court ruled George W. Bush to be the Supreme Ruler of the country for all time.

OBERGEFELL v. HODGES

All they wanted was to be gay-married. That's it. Nothing else. There is no slippery slope!

What will happen if gay marriage is legalized?

- Gay people will get married
- A third world war will break
- The terrorists will win

MARBURY v. MADISON

Granted courts additional power, similar to how Jar Jar Binks expanded the powers of Chancellor Palpatine.

PLESSY v. FERGUSON

Upheld racial segregation. Was at one time settled law of the land, much like Roe v. Wade currently is.

Batman v. Superman: DAWN OF JUSTICE - The Snyder Cut, Fullscreen, Like NEW - $19.99 OBO

★★★☆☆ 2 product ratings

Condition: Brand New

Price: US $19.99

Buy It Now

Add to cart

♡ Add to Watchlist

Ships from United States

Pickup: Free local pickup available See details
Shipping: $3.19 Economy Shipping | See details
Returns: Seller does not accept returns | See details
Payments: PayPal G Pay VISA

Shop with confidence

eBay Money Back Guarantee
Get the item you ordered or get your money back.
Learn more

Seller information
DanDillon(82)
100% Positive feedback

♡ Save this seller
Contact seller
See other items

$ Have one to sell? Sell now

(LESSER-KNOWN SUPREME COURT CASES)

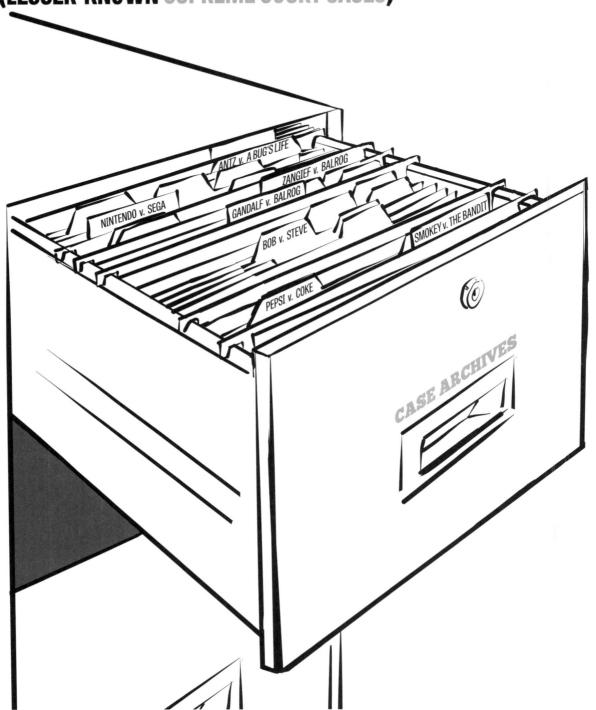

HOTDOGS v. SANDWICHES

THE PEOPLE
v.
THE NEW SONIC
THE HEDGEHOG
DESIGN

WHITE & GOLD
v.
BLACK & BLUE

PEWDIEPIE v. T-SERIES

PINEAPPLE PIZZA v. NORMAL PIZZA

UNFORSEEN v. SLOPPY WET KISS

SCOTT PILGRIM v. THE WORLD

JOEL OSTEEN v. THE BIBLE

IT'S TIME TO GET BORKED

In 1987, President Ronald Reagan nominated Robert Bork to replace Lewis Powell Jr. on the Supreme Court. Up to that point in history, most Supreme Court justices were appointed to their positions through a fairly routine confirmation process, with exceptions in any cases when severe controversy in the judge's past would prohibit them from serving justly.

How lame is that?!

But with Bork, things got a lot more exciting, and Supreme Court nominations became the circus the Founding Fathers intended them to be. The nomination of Robert Bork allowed the Democrats to come up with the brilliant idea of dragging up any kind of accusation, no matter how false, to try to stop a nominee they didn't like.

Hey, at least Supreme Court nominations are exciting now!

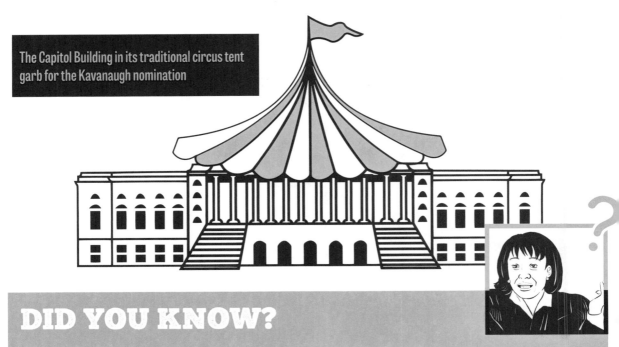

The Capitol Building in its traditional circus tent garb for the Kavanaugh nomination

DID YOU KNOW?

President Joe Biden has opposed not one, but two black Supreme Court Justice contenders: **Clarence Thomas** and **Janice Rogers Brown**. Biden led the charge in actively borking Thomas's nomination and threatened to kill Brown's potential nomination if she was ever considered. He was simply paving the way for his future historic token black SCOTUS pick: child pornography defender **Ketanji Brown Jackson**.

THE MOST BORKED NOMINEES OF ALL TIME

Ever since Bork, most nominees get borked. It's borking all the way down! Here are the most-borked SCOTUS nominees in history:

BORK

Was opposed for his dangerous video rental history after it was discovered he had rented *Cannonball Run 2* from a local Blockbuster.

RICK AKERMAN

A little-known SCOTUS nominee from the Cleveland administration. He turned out to be three racoons stacked on top of each other in a trenchcoat.

THOMAS

Democrats attacked Clarence Thomas by digging up a sexual assault allegation from Anita Hill. It was totally not because Joe Biden has a weird thing against black people.

ACB

Democrats tried to torpedo Amy Coney Barrett's nomination by accusing her of being too Catholic, having too many kids, and being too pretty.

KAVANAUGH

Democrats dragged up several accusers to claim Brett Kavanaugh enjoyed beer in high school.

BORKING REASONS

As you can see, you don't need a real good reason to bork someone. So, to save time and effort, we've provided a full page of reasons you can bork someone. Just flip a coin onto the open page, and whatever item the coin lands closest to will be just about as legitimate a reason as any historical borking.

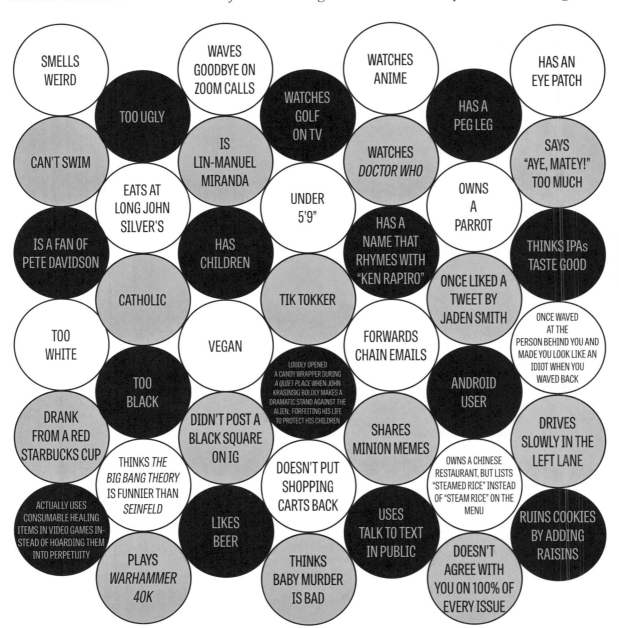

HOW PRESIDENTS NOMINATE A SUPREME COURT JUSTICE

REPUBLICAN PRESIDENTS ASK

What is their judicial history?

Are they competent?

Do they interpret the law as written without inserting their own politics into their rulings?

Do they own at least twenty-seven firearms?

How much do they like beer?

Is this the best person for our agenda?

DEMOCRAT PRESIDENTS ASK

Do they want to kill babies?

Will they ignore the law and rule according to the prevailing left-wing doctrine?

What color is their skin?

What gender are they?

Do they really want to kill babies???

Is this the best person for our agenda?

INTERACTING WITH THE JUSTICE SYSTEM:
WHAT TO DO WHEN YOU GET PULLED OVER

It's scary to see those flashing red and blue lights in your rearview mirror. Getting pulled over is sure to kick your adrenal glands into full gear, and we don't always act rationally when our body is in a state of fight or flight. Therefore, it's good to have a strategy going into any police interactions you may have.

Hold your hand up to this graph. If your skintone falls to the left of the arrow, read instructions from Column A. If your skintone falls to the right of the arrow, read instructions from Column B.

COLUMN A	COLUMN B
• Procure your ID and registration and place them in a visible location on the dashboard.	• Do whatever you want.
• Roll down your window, then place both hands on the steering wheel.	• Spit in the officer's face while screaming indignantly.
• Address the officer politely, and acknowledge everything he says with a smile.	• Insult the officer's appearance while making pig noises.
• Thank the officer for his service.	• Ask, "Do you know who my father is!?"
• Prepare to get shot.	• Back your car into their car while laughing maniacally.
	• Get away scot-free, since the system was built to benefit you.

Aside from these general guidelines, here are some tried-and-true strategies for interacting with the police and hopefully avoiding the long arm of the justice system:

HOW TO GET OUT OF A TICKET

Incapacitate with Pocket Sand

It's super effective!

Cry

Weep, ye mortals, and get out of a ticket.

Be a Cute Girl

It's the easiest way to escape the consequences of your own actions.

Say You're Holding These Two Tons of Cocaine for Your Friend, Steve

Oh, THIS cocaine? It's Steve's! Classic Steve!

HOW TO GET OUT OF A TICKET

Shout "AM I BEING DETAINED?"

Also works during church greeting time.

Summon the Murder Hornets

They can be summoned with the power of your hea[rt]

Explain the Plot of *Tenet* until Cop Falls Asleep

"And so the different colored armbands differentiate the direction that time flows . . ."

Deploy Boom Box Blasting Nicki Minaj

Get him super-bassed as you stay super-based.

Tell the Cop That You Are WHITE

Then carry on with your day.

HOW TO WIN A COURT CASE: TIPS FOR ATTORNEYS

I SAW THE RIOT FIRSTHAND. IT WAS MOSTLY PEACEFUL.

LOOK FOR INCONSISTENCIES

Review the witness testimony line by line.

YELL "OBJECTION!"

When you find an inconsistency in the testimony, shout, **"OBJECTION!"** at the top of your lungs while pointing at the witness in an accusatory fashion.

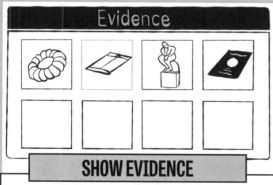

Evidence

SHOW EVIDENCE

Display to the court how a piece of evidence in your possession contradicts the witness's testimony.

LOSING LIFE

If you fail to present the proper evidence, your life meter in the upper right corner will deplete. If your life drops to zero, it's a guilty verdict for your client, and a GAME OVER for you.

PRESENT EVIDENCE AND TURN THE TIDE OF BATTLE IN YOUR FAVOR!

MUSEUM OF JUSTICE

As we conclude our tour of the justice system, let's take a stroll through the museum of justice. From Justice Earl Warren's head preserved in a jar to the gavel Justice Sonia Sotomayor got stuck in her nose—again—you'll be in awe of our democracy's judicial branch as you wander these hallowed halls. Just stay close, and don't touch anything. Especially that gavel.

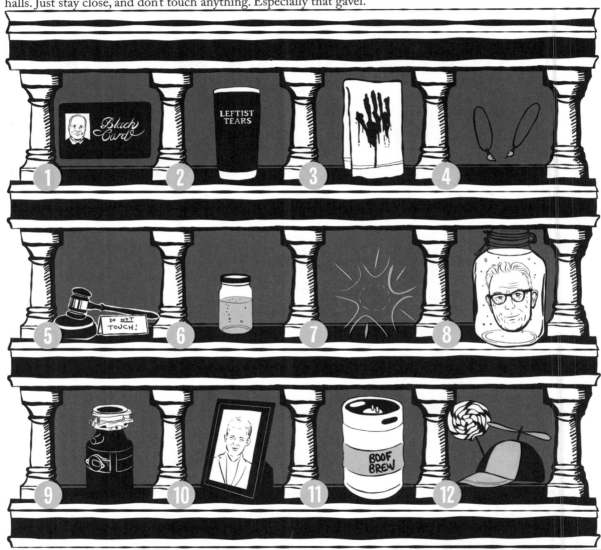

1. Clarence Thomas's Black Card that he lost when he deigned to think for himself
2. Tumbler holding Christine Blasey Ford's fake tears
3. The blood on the hands of the justices from sixty million babies killed
4. Scalia and RGB's friendship bracelets
5. The gavel Sonia Sotomayor got stuck in her nose. Again.
6. Chief Justice John Roberts's liquified spine
7. The emanations of the penumbra surrounding the right to privacy
8. Justice Earl Warren's head preserved in a jar
9. An illegal garbage disposal sent back from a time when Chief Justice AOC has outlawed them
10. ACB's favorite child
11. Brett Kavanaugh's favorite keg
12. The lollipop and spinner cap Joseph Story had on him when he was confirmed

CHAPTER REVIEW: THE JUDICIAL BRANCH

We've discussed so many incredible things in these last few pages. Let's take a minute to check our comprehension for absolutely no reason whatsoever.

1. Where do you need judgment in your life?

2. Have you accepted Brett Kavanaugh as your lord and savior? Why or why not?

3. Thomas Jefferson opposed the concept of judicial review, in which the federal courts could strike down federal and state laws, on the basis that it would make the Constitution "a mere thing of wax in the hands of the judiciary, which they may twist and shape into any form they may please" and that it "would place us under the despotism of an oligarchy." Since cases like Marbury v. Madison and Roe v. Wade, the Supreme Court has decided that it is such an oligarchy. What federal or state law do you think the Supreme Court should strike down next, or what new right do you think the Supreme Court should invent out of whole cloth, like the right to abortion? Explain your answer in the space below.

4. Have you ever been borked? Explain.

5. Did you touch the gavel? Why did you do that?

Chapter 6

The Corporate Branch

Walmart Amazon Apple CVS Health UnitedHealth Group Berkshire Hathaway McKesson AmerisourceBergen Alphabet Exxon Mobil AT&T Costco Wholesale Cigna Cardinal Health Microsoft Walgreens Boots Alliance Kroger Home Depot JPMorgan Chase Verizon Communications Ford Motor General Motors Anthem Centene Fannie Mae Comcast Chevron Dell Technologies Bank of America Target Lowe's Marathon Petroleum Citigroup Facebook UPS Johnson & Johnson Wells Fargo General Electric State Farm Insurance Intel Humana IBM Procter & Gamble PepsiCo FedEx MetLife Freddie Mac Phillips 66 Lockheed Martin Walt Disney Archer Daniels Midland Valero Energy Boeing Prudential Financial HP Raytheon Technologies StoneX Group Goldman Sachs Group Sysco Morgan Stanley HCA Healthcare Cisco Systems Charter Communications Merck Best Buy New York Life Insurance AbbVie Publix Super Markets Allstate Liberty Mutual Insurance Group AIG Tyson Foods Progressive Bristol-Myers Squibb Nationwide Pfizer Caterpillar TIAA Oracle Energy Transfer Dow American Express General Dynamics Nike Northrop Grumman USAA Deere Abbott Laboratories Northwestern Mutual Dollar General Exelon Coca-Cola Honeywell International Thermo Fisher Scientific 3M TJX Travelers Capital One Financial Tesla Philip Morris International Electronics CHS Jabil Enterprise Products Partners Hewlett Packard Enterprise United Natural Foods Mondelez International ViacomCBS Kraft Heinz Dollar Tree Amgen U.S. Bancorp Performance Food Group Netflix Gilead Sciences Synnex Eli Lilly Truist Financial PNC Financial Services Group Broadcom CBRE Group Massachusetts Mutual Life Insurance Qualcomm Starbucks Duke Energy Plains GP Holdings US Foods Holding Lennar Dollar Rite Aid Visa PayPal Holdings Micron Technology CarMax Salesforce Altria Group Lumen Technologies Baker Hughes International Paper Hartford Financial Services Group PG&E Group DuPont AutoNation Northern World Fuel Services D.R. Horton Nucor Cummins NGL Energy Partners DXC Technology Union Pacific Whirlpool Molina Healthcare Conagra McDonald's Kimberly-Clark Parker CSX CDW Sherwin-Williams L3Harris Technologies Macy's ManpowerGroup Tenet Healthcare Avnet General Mills WestRock Carrier Global Aramark Genuine Parts Applied Materials Becton Dickinson Delta Air Lines Lear Bank of New York Mellon Emerson Electric Western Digital Occidental Petroleum Nvidia Cognizant Technology Jones Lang LaSalle Synchrony Financial Colgate-Palmolive AECOM XPO Logistics C.H. Robinson Worldwide BlackRock Dominion Energy Rocket Companies Kohl's Fluor DISH Network United Airlines Holdings Mastercard Waste Management PBF Energy American Electric Power Fiserv Principal Financial Reinsurance Group of America Automatic Data Processing Stanley Black & Decker Texas Instruments Halliburton Stryker Estée Lauder Corteva Freeport-McMoRan Qurate Retail Wayfair Laboratory Corp. of America Land O'Lakes PPG Industries Gap Kellogg Hershey-Hormel Whole-Mart Holding Jacobs Engineering Group Edison International Guardian Life Ins. Co. of America Biogen Omnicom Group Unum Group Lithia Motors American Family Insurance Group Financial Services Adobe Otis Worldwide Ecolab AutoZone Loews Illinois Tool Works Fidelity National Information Services Ross Stores Peter Kiewit Sons' Equitable International Goodyear Tire & Rubber Fox Leidos Holdings Consolidated Edison DTE Energy Charles Schwab State Street Ameriprise Financial Viatris Sempra Energy Exchange L Brands W.W. Grainger Community Health Systems Ball Berry Global Group Kinder Morgan VF International Textron Keurig Dr Pepper Holdings Universal Health Services DaVita Xcel Energy Newmont Vistra IQVIA Holdings eBay Corning Quanta Services HollyFrontier Bed Bath & Beyond Omaha Insurance Conagra Brands PulteGroup EOG Resources Group 1 Automotive Ally Financial Fidelity National Financial Northern Trust Discovery FirstEnergy Jones Financial (Edward Jones) BorgWarner Republic Services Henry Schein Expeditors of Washington Research Boston Scientific Altice USA Norfolk Southern Sonic Automotive Advanced Micro Devices United Continental Holdings Support Services KKR Hormel Foods Public Service Enterprise Group Steel Dynamics Dick's Sporting Goods Mohawk Industries Washington International Ingalls Industries Cheniere Energy SpartanNash Alcoa AGCO Voya Financial NRG Energy Interpublic Group Energy Alleghany Air Products & Chemicals Auto-Owners Insurance CenterPoint Energy Reliance Steel & Aluminum TechFinancial Amphenol Builders FirstSource Oneok United Rentals Brighthouse Financial Regeneron Pharmaceuticals Third Constellation Brands Insight Enterprises Global Partners US Solutions Yum China Holdings James Thor Industries Thrivent Financial for Lutherans Hershey's Casey's General Stores W.R. Berkley American Financial Group Darden Restaurants J.M. Smucker Western Citizens Financial Weyerhaeuser West Chemical Navistar International Hamilton Holding Au Motorola Solutions Graybar Electric Energy Group Old Republic International Communications Group Seaboard Toll Brothers Applications International Group Roofing Financial Group Oshkosh Financial Graphic Packaging PriceVertex Pharmaceutical Enterprises O-1 Huntsman ABM Industries International Arconic

If you went to a dumb public school, you probably think there are only three branches of government. Boy, are you dumb!

"You are so DUMB,

You are really DUMB.

FOR REAL."

Antoine Dodson
EXPERT ON DUMBNESS

There are actually at least four branches of government.

The fourth branch in our glorious American democracy is the corporate branch.

The corporate branch is not in the Constitution—at least, not in the first draft. According to legend, the corporate branch was added to a top-secret second draft of the Constitution by the Chamber of Commerce hundreds of years ago.

Since the government is staffed mostly by people with low IQs and severe mental health problems, they need big powerful corporations to help them run everything. Corporations in turn need the help of the government. The government has guns, and it can use those guns to help crush a corporation's competition and help make the company more money in a miraculous democratic process called

"CRONY CAPITALISM."

CRONY CAPITALISM: THE GREAT PARTNERSHIP OF DEMOCRACY

Here's how it works:

POLITICIAN GETS	CEO GETS
Unlimited wealth	Protection from regulations
Political support from powerful CEOs	Favorable tax laws
Help running the country	Government power to crush small business competition
Free steak dinner	Free steak dinner
Free prostitutes	Free prostitutes

Between the corporations, a deeply entrenched regulatory state, corrupt politicians, and lobbyists, you have a highly effective shadow government that greatly benefits the corporations, a deeply entrenched regulatory state, corrupt politicians, and lobbyists. Neat!

CEOS: THE LEADERS OF THE FOURTH BRANCH OF GOVERNMENT

CEOs are smarter than politicians. They also provide jobs and create innovations that lift up the poor in surprising new ways. Unfortunately, they are also richer than us, which makes them totally evil.

CEOs also are often tempted by the power government wields against their competition, are prone to using corrupt practices to keep the government from bothering them, and will sometimes sacrifice doing the right thing to make more money. In short, they're wonderful people.

CEOs: A CLOSER LOOK

MONOCLE
To examine their gold coins

CELL PHONE
Senator on speed dial

CHINESE CHARACTER TATTOO
From business trip to Thailand;
it actually doesn't mean what he
thinks it means

"SOCIAL JUSTICE" T-SHIRT
Made by Uyghur slaves

**"BLACK LIVES MATTER"
BRANDED CAVIAR**
Delicious and organic

REMNANTS OF ACQUSITIONS
So many startups
destroyed

TOP HAT
Made from baby seals

BLACK, EMPTY VOID
Where heart used to be,
now covered by rainbow
heart pin

BINDER FULL OF WOMEN
Ripe for exploiting at 79
cents on the dollar

GIANT BAG OF MONEY
For bribing his senator

FAMOUS CEOs

JEFF BEZOS
Amazon, and soon the world.

SIR PETER WEYLAND
Weyland Corporation

HIDEO YUTANI
Weyland-Yutani Corporation

MARK ZUCKERBERG
(definitely not a lizard)
~~Facebook~~ META

TIM APPLE
Cook Inc.

**CRYOGENICALLY FROZEN
BILL GATES**
Microsoft, and a whole bunch
of farmland for some reason

THE PARTS OF THE CORPORATE BRANCH

Just like the other branches of government, the corporate branch is comprised of many different moving parts to make sure the whole thing keeps running smoothly and making tons of money. Err—rather, to serve man. That's what they do. All good folks running the major corporations. Public servants, really. Alexa is listening please send help.

Everything is great under the corporate branch!

Let's take a look now at how it's all organized. From Big Tech and Big Oil to fan favorites like Big Pharma, the corporate branch is filled with everyone's favorite giant corporations, wriggling their way into every aspect of our lives like tentacles.

Hey, that'd be a great illustration! Turn the page and you'll see.

THE PARTS OF THE CORPORATE BRANCH

Big Tech

From the heart of Mordor, a great eye sits atop a dark tower, watching your every move, hearing your every word, penetrating your very thoughts. The oligarchs of Big Tech are here to make sure you have no unacceptable opinions as they monetize your hopes, dreams, and your innermost soul. They also help the government get around the Bill of Rights by censoring all the speech the government doesn't like. Relax, this is for your own good.

Big Oil

Every day, fat men with cigars gather in a smoke-filled room and conspire about new ways to rape the earth for precious natural resources so you can drive cars, use air conditioning, and toast your bread. Pure evil.

Big Entertainment

A union of Disney, Netflix, and Amazon designed to pipe pretty pictures into your brain so you're not paying attention to the fact that they're probably diddling kids.

Big Food

You will eat the processed food. You will consume the sugar. And Big Food will be there in Washington, D.C., to ensure the status quo never changes.

Big Scented Candle

Every week, the titans of Big Scented Candle conspire about new ways to lure your wife into their stores and fool her into paying outrageous prices for their infernal candles. They must be stopped.

Big Satire

Russia pays thousands of joke writers and meme makers to spread deadly misinformation under the guise of satire. Thankfully, they are opposed by the heroes at Big Fact Check.

Big Pharma

The lobbyists of Big Pharma have a dedicated wing of the Capitol Building where they are hard at work making up new diseases so they can sell new drugs that create new diseases for which they can sell new drugs. They're just following the science!

The Corporate Media

The corporate media is completely trustworthy. They protect our democracy. They will always tell the truth. Repeat this ten times.

Military Industrial Complex

A cabal of brilliant engineers and salespeople who are always coming up with new ways to kill people drinking chai at a cafe in Yemen using an Xbox controller in California.

Big Mask

The corporate heroes at Big Mask convince the other branches of government to pass laws saying everyone has to buy masks. Wear one, two, or even seven masks to show that you support Big Mask.

HOW THE CORPORATE BRANCH PROTECTS ITSELF

To keep everyone off the trail of their sordid dealings, corporations use very special techniques to make themselves look like the good guys so no one will interfere. On any given day, the corporate branch is engaged in bribing government officials, exploiting loopholes in government regulations, employing slave labor in China, and creating unbearable commercials to interrupt your YouTube videos. Pretty nasty stuff!

To distract everyone from all this, corporations employ an effective defensive technique called "wokeness," like a squid that shoots ink to evade a predator. As long as a company is saying all the right things publicly, and bribes all the right politicians privately, they are generally free to do what they want.

THE CORPORATE MEDIA:
THE WATCHFUL PROTECTORS OF DEMOCRACY

In spite of all the corruption and wickedness of government/corporate partnerships, there is one corporate entity that is incorruptible: the corporate media!

The corporate media are the watchful protectors of our glorious democracy. They make sure we know everything we should know, and don't know anything we shouldn't know, because they know what's best for us. They never lie or stretch the truth to fit an agenda. They are the watchmen our democracy needs!

But who watches the watchmen, you ask? Sorry, we don't understand the question. You're so silly!

Since the media always tells the truth, you can always count on them to get all the accurate news you need to stand up for democracy!

Unfortunately, sometimes they use words and phrases that make them difficult to understand.

This is because they are highly educated and have a strong vocabulary.

How will you ever keep up? Well, don't worry! We prepared this special translation guide just for you, so the next time you're watching the news you'll be able to follow along!

Turn to the next page to see!

HANDY DANDY CORPORATE MEDIA TRANSLATION GUIDE

WHAT THEY SAID	WHAT THEY ACTUALLY MEANT
"DEBUNKED CONSPIRACY THEORY"	A COMPLETELY FACTUAL EVENT THAT IS 100% TRUE AND WE DON'T LIKE IT
"THIS IS DANGEROUS MISINFORMATION"	WE DON'T REALLY AGREE WITH IT BUT PEOPLE ARE STILL SHARING IT
"FARM ANIMAL BACTERIAL INFECTION TREATMENT"	PENICILLIN
"CONSERVATIVE PANELIST"	GUY WHO ONCE VOTED FOR RONALD REAGAN, POSSIBLY BY MISTAKE
"SUPERSPREADER EVENT"	GATHERINGS OF PEOPLE WE DON'T LIKE
"THIS IS THE END OF DEMOCRACY"	TRUMP SAID A THING
"SETTLED SCIENCE"	A NON-REVIEWED STUDY BY A POSSIBLY FICTITIOUS ORGANIZATION THAT JUST CAME OUT THIS MORNING
"WIDESPREAD OUTRAGE"	THREE PEOPLE ON TWITTER GOT MAD
"RACIST STATEMENTS"	LITERALLY MEANS NOTHING

HANDY DANDY CORPORATE MEDIA TRANSLATION GUIDE

WHAT THEY SAID	WHAT THEY ACTUALLY MEANT
"INFORMAL GATHERING OF LIKE-MINDED PEOPLE THAT FOSTERS A SENSE OF CAMARADERIE AND COMMUNITY AMONG FRIENDS AND NEIGHBORS"	BREAD LINES
"ZERO"	ANY NUMBER FROM ZERO TO SEVERAL TRILLION
"REPUBLICANS POUNCE"	UH OH . . . A DEMOCRAT RAPED SOMEONE
"MOSTLY PEACEFUL"	IT WAS HYPER-VIOLENT BUT WE AGREE WITH IT
"RACIST DOG WHISTLE"	A SUPER-SECRET WHISTLE THAT ONLY RACISTS CAN HEAR AND ONLY WE HEARD IT
"ANONYMOUS SOURCES"	WE TOTALLY MADE THIS UP

GETTING YOUR TRUTH FROM THE RIGHT SOURCES:

If you need to know what's going on, there are only two sources available: Fox News and CNN. As far as we know, there are no other sources. It's important to get balanced news by watching both sources all the time. If you watch only one, your worldview will be skewed and you won't be smart enough to defend democracy. To make sure you're not watching too much of one or the other, follow this handy guide:

SIGNS YOU'RE WATCHING TOO MUCH CNN

You think the pandemic is still going on. If you find yourself saying, "When the pandemic is over . . ." or "the new normal," you might be watching too much CNN.

You still think one of these investigations is going to "get" Trump.
The walls are closing in. Any day now.

You haven't left your house in two years.
Time to turn off the CNN and go outside, people.

You haven't heard of any of Biden's foreign or domestic failures. You think the president's doing a "pretty good job" and haven't caught wind of any kind of disasters.

You still call ivermectin "horse medicine." Oh no!
Your brain has been infected!

You walk by a fiery riot and think to yourself, "Ah, what a peaceful protest. Mostly, anyway." If this is your immediate instinct, check with a medical professional. You may have an oversaturation of CNN.

You're at the airport a lot. This is less a symptom and more a root cause, but if you're at the airport, you're probably watching lots of CNN.

You drop to the floor and convulse any time you see a MAGA hat.
The longer you roll around in the fetal position, the more CNN you probably watch.

You watch any CNN at all. Even one second is too much.
Just say no.

SIGNS YOU'RE WATCHING TOO MUCH FOX NEWS

You give your wife the "Tucker Carlson look" while she's talking.
If you've ever gotten in trouble for staring at your wife with Carlson's patented
Resting Baffled Face™, you might be watching too much Fox News.

You start thinking maybe you need SeaBond denture cream.
Those commercials start to sound pretty good late at night.

Sean Hannity is starting to look attractive.
Oh no. Turn it off immediately!

The other people in the old folks' home say, "Hey, Gilbert! Turn off the Fox News already!"
If your fellow members of the Greatest Generation think you're watching too much,
turn the ol' tube off and go play some shuffleboard.

You instinctively add the phrase "May He Live Forever"
every time you say "Donald Trump." Like a kneejerk reaction.

Your crazy uncle's rants at Thanksgiving are starting to make a lot of sense. You start
thinking, "You know what? Uncle Fred actually makes some really good points."

You're not aware of a single good thing Biden has done. Well, to be fair . . .

You call everything you don't like "woke" or "cancel culture." Morning traffic? Woke.
Decaf coffee? Cancel culture! Marvel movies? Woke AND cancel culture!

Your bedroom pillow, your throw pillows, and your couch cushions are all MyPillows.
Oh no! You've been brainwashed!

MEET YOUR CORPORATE OVERLORDS

DISNEY
Makes movies, cartoons, and theme parks for all ages.

FUN FACT:
An army of robot Mickey Mouses is housed in the tunnels under Disneyland.

NIKE
Makes shoes and shirts. Well, its child laborers do.

FUN FACT:
Custom signature Amy Schumer Nikes are coming this fall.

NETFLIX
Streams shows exclusively featuring gay BIPOC characters.

FUN FACT:
When *The Office* left Netflix there was literally nothing left to watch here.

APPLE
Makes smartphones and computers. Well, its child laborers do.

FUN FACT:
Apple once put out a box of nothing and sold it for $999. It sold out instantly.

TWITTER
A platform for free speech as long as Twitter agrees with it.

FUN FACT:
The Taliban was once banned from Twitter for sharing a Babylon Bee joke.

FACEBOOK
A social network that only grandmas still use.

FUN FACT:

Your church just learned how to create a Facebook page three months ago.

AMAZON
An online storefront that will soon take over the world.

FUN FACT:

CEO Jeff Bezos sometimes gets drunk and orders stuff from his own site.

WALMART
A store filled with fun, smiling employees and great smells.

FUN FACT:

Walmart has implemented a must-wear-pants mandate in all its stores.

LOCKHEED MARTIN
Manufacturer of fun things we use in wars.

FUN FACT:

Chants of "War! War! War!" can often be heard coming from its offices.

GOOGLE
A search engine/world domination company.

FUN FACT:

Google quietly removed "Don't" from its "Don't Be Evil" slogan in 2017.

REMEMBER: THE CORPORATIONS ARE ALWAYS RIGHT

As you flipped through these pages of our beloved American megacorporations, we hope you were filled with warm, fuzzy feelings toward our corporate overlords. Because if you weren't feeling sufficient levels of happiness, well, we regret to inform you that your Apple Watch detected your apathy and Amazon has dispatched an attack drone to your home to take care of you. Sorry!

You should have fostered in yourself sufficient love for the Party that rules you.

Remember: our glorious utopian future is a future in which the corporations are always right.

ALL HAIL THE CORPORATIONS

WOW!

All hail the great and mighty corporations who rule us. Let's take a tour now through the sacred Museum of Corporations so you can gain more insight into our glorious corporate overlords. Just remember, by entering the Museum of Corporations, you surrender your right to free speech, personhood, privacy, life, detainment, trial, innocence before being proven guilty, movement, seek a safe place to live, nationality, marriage, family, to own things, thought, expression, public assembly, democracy, Social Security, worker's rights, to play, food and shelter, education, copyright, fair and free world, responsibility, free speech, personhood, privacy, life, detainment, trial, innocence before being proven guilty, movement, seek a safe place to live, nationality, marriage, family, to own things, thought, expression, public assembly, democracy, Social Security, worker's rights, to play, food and shelter, education, copyright, fair and free world, responsibility, free speech, personhood, privacy, life, detainment, trial, innocence before being proven guilty, movement, seek a safe place to live, nationality, marriage, family, to own things, thought, expression, public assembly, democracy, Social Security, worker's rights, to play, food and shelter, education, copyright, fair and free world, responsibility, free speech, personhood, privacy, life, detainment, trial, innocence before being proven guilty, movement, seek a safe place to live, nationality, marriage, family, to own things, thought, expression, public assembly, democracy, Social Security, worker's rights, to play, food and shelter, education, copyright, fair and free world, responsibility, free speech, personhood, privacy, life, detainment, trial, innocence before being proven guilty, movement, seek a safe place to live, nationality, marriage, family, to own things, thought, expression, public assembly, democracy, Social Security, worker's rights, to play, food and shelter, education, copyright, fair and free world, responsibility, free speech, personhood, privacy, life, detainment, trial, innocence before being proven guilty, movement, seek a safe place to live, nationality, marriage, family, to own things, thought, expression, public assembly, democracy, Social Security, worker's rights, to play, food and shelter, education, copyright, fair and free world, responsibility, free speech, personhood, privacy, life, detainment, trial, innocence before being proven guilty, movement, seek a safe place to live, nationality, marriage, family, to own things, thought, expression, public assembly, democracy, Social Security, worker's rights, to play, food and shelter, education, copyright, fair and free world, responsibility, free speech, personhood, privacy, life, detainment, trial, innocence before being proven guilty, movement, seek a safe place to live, nationality, marriage, family, to own things, thought, expression, public assembly, democracy, Social Security, worker's rights, to play, food and shelter, education, copyright, fair and free world, responsibility, free speech, personhood, privacy, life, detainment, trial, innocence before being proven guilty, movement, seek a safe place to live, nationality, marriage, family, to own things, thought, expression, public assembly, democracy, Social Security, worker's rights, to play, food and shelter, education, copyright, fair and free world, responsibility, free speech, personhood, privacy, life, detainment, trial, innocence before being proven guilty, movement, seek a safe place to live, nationality, marriage, family, to own things, thought, expression, public assembly, democracy, Social Security, worker's rights, to play, food and shelter, education, copyright, fair and free world, responsibility, free speech, personhood, privacy, life, detainment, trial, innocence before being proven guilty, movement, seek a safe place to live, nationality, marriage, family, to own things, thought, expression, public assembly, democracy, Social Security, worker's rights, to play, food and shelter, education, copyright, fair and free world, responsibility, free speech, personhood, privacy, life, detainment, trial, innocence before being proven guilty, movement, seek a safe place to live, nationality, marriage, family, to own things, thought, expression, public assembly, democracy, Social Security, worker's rights, to play, food and shelter, education, copyright, fair and free world, responsibility, free speech, personhood, privacy, life, detainment, trial, innocence before being proven guilty, movement, seek a safe place to live, nationality, marriage, family, to own things, thought, expression, public assembly, democracy, Social Security, worker's rights, to play, food and shelter, education, copyright, fair and free world, responsibility, free speech, personhood, privacy, life, detainment, trial, innocence before being proven guilty, movement, seek a safe place to live, nationality, marriage, family, to own things, thought, expression, public assembly, democracy, Social Security, worker's rights, to play, food and shelter, education, copyright, fair and free world, responsibility, free speech, personhood, privacy, life, detainment, trial, innocence before being proven guilty, movement, seek a safe place to live, nationality, marriage, family, to own things, thought, expression, public assembly, democracy, Social Security, worker's rights, to play, food and shelter, education, copyright, fair and free world, responsibility, free speech, personhood, privacy, life, detainment, trial, innocence before being proven guilty, movement, seek a safe place to live, nationality, marriage, family, to own things, thought, expression, public assembly, democracy, Social Security, worker's rights, to play, food and shelter, education, copyright, fair and free world, responsibility, free speech, personhood, privacy, life, detainment, trial, innocence before being proven guilty, movement, seek a safe place to live, nationality, marriage, family, to own things, thought, expression, public assembly, democracy, Social Security, worker's rights, to play, food and shelter, education, copyright, fair and free world, responsibility, free speech, personhood, privacy, life, detainment, trial, innocence before being proven guilty, movement, seek a safe place to live, nationality, marriage, family, to own things, thought, expression, public assembly, democracy, Social Security, worker's rights, to play, food and shelter, education, copyright, fair and free world, responsibility, free speech, personhood, privacy, life, detainment, trial, innocence before being proven guilty, movement, seek a safe place to live, nationality, marriage, family, to own things, thought, expression, public assembly, democracy, Social Security, worker's rights, to play, food and shelter, education, copyright, fair and free world, responsibility, free speech, personhood, privacy, life, detainment, trial, innocence before being proven guilty, movement, seek a safe place to live, nationality, marriage, family, to own things, thought, expression, public assembly, democracy, Social Security, worker's rights, to play, food and shelter, education, copyright, fair and free world, responsibility, free speech, personhood, privacy, life, detainment, trial, innocence before being proven guilty, movement, seek a safe place to live, nationality, marriage, family, to own things, thought, expression, public assembly, democracy, Social Security, worker's rights, to play, food and shelter, education, copyright, fair and free world, responsibility, free speech, personhood, privacy, life, detainment, trial, innocence before being proven guilty, movement, etc...

MUSEUM OF CORPORATIONS

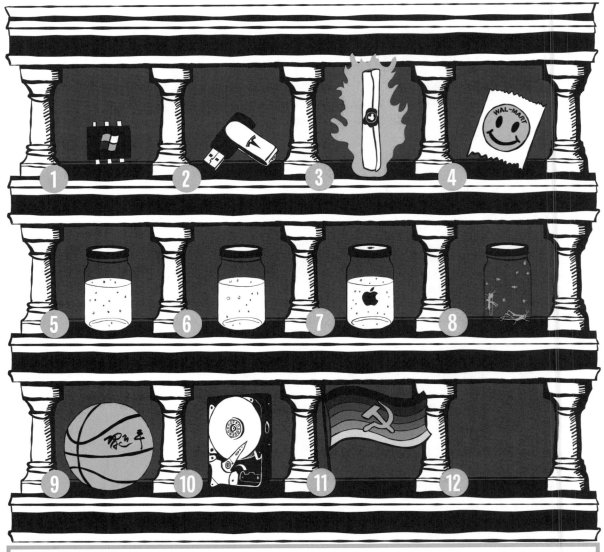

1. The microchip Bill Gates puts into the vaccines
2. Elon Musk's first-ever meme
3. Copy of contract Disney signed with Satan to brainwash all the children
4. First Walmart happy face sticker handed out by an old man at the front doors in 1972
5. Sweat of exploited Amazon worker in jar
6. Sweat of exploited Nike child laborers in jar
7. Sweat of exploited Apple factory worker in jar (on sale at Apple store for $299)
8. Mark Zuckerberg's lunchtime snack of flies and locusts
9. NBA basketball signed by all-star Xi Jinping
10. Google hard drive with all your private information on it
11. Pride/Communism flag hanging at Twitter headquarters
12. Every major corporation's integrity and love for America

CHAPTER REVIEW: THE CORPORATE BRANCH

We've discussed so many incredible things in these last few pages. Let's take a minute to check our comprehension for absolutely no reason whatsoever.

1. Do you welcome our corporate overlords? And remember, Alexa is always listening.

2. Will you commit in this very moment to bow to Mickey Mouse?

3. If you were forced to watch one for all eternity, would you watch CNN or Fox News?

4. Did you spot Benjamin Franklin Gates in this chapter, defending our democracy?

5. Patrick Deneed has written much about the advance of anticulture that is the "consequence of a universal and homogenous market, resulting in a monoculture that colonizes and destroys actual cultures rooted in experience, history, and place" and how the "wedding" between global corporations and anti-human agendas and ideologies is not surprising. In the space provided, please explain how global corporations like Disney getting special favors from the State are actually good for a thriving and strong citizenry's values, traditions, and local community.

6. Don't let the corporations distract you from the fact that in 1998, The Undertaker threw Mankind off Hell in a Cell, and plummeted sixteen feet through an announcer's table.

Chapter 7

Know Your
Constitutional Rights

As you read through this book, you might be asking yourself, "Steve,[1] this government is starting to sound really big and bloated. What's to prevent the feds from just trampling all over my rights, throwing me in jail, taking my guns, and forcing me to quarter soldiers in my home?"

That's a great question, Steve.[2]

It's time to tell you about a magic piece of paper called "The Constitution."

The Constitution is a document of genius designed to restrain the power of government and guarantee the rights of the people. It used to project a powerful force field that physically kept the government in check, but over time the force field stopped working and now the government is just on the honor system. The document is now housed behind bulletproof glass in the National Archives, where legislators periodically visit and double check what it says so they can ignore it.

[1] If your name is Steve, of course.
[2] See footnote 1.

THE CONSTITUTION: KNOW YOUR RIGHTS

The Founders believed your rights come from nature and nature's God, and not from government. The Constitution is just there to enumerate the rights that are already yours. Hey—wake up—are you still listening?

This is important!

The Constitution created a federal government to unify the states and protect individual rights through a series of checks and balances. To this day, America's Constitution is the world's most successful and enduring political document ever written. This is because—

Hey! You're falling asleep! Don't fall asleep, you're going to miss some important history here!

So, as we were saying, the Constitution has endured due to the amazing ability of American citizens to self-govern. This is because, for many years, Americans have been a God-fearing people who have a reason for living righteously that transcends the law. Founder John Adams said it best when he said, "Our Constitution was made only for a moral and religious people. It is wholly inadequate to the government of any other." To the extent the core of the American people remains religious and moral, the Constitution will endure. This is why it's so important to—

Wow. You're actually snoring now. OK, what's it gonna take to keep your attention? Do you want a picture?

OK—here's a picture:

Well, maybe something a little more on-topic.

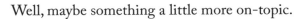

You awake now?

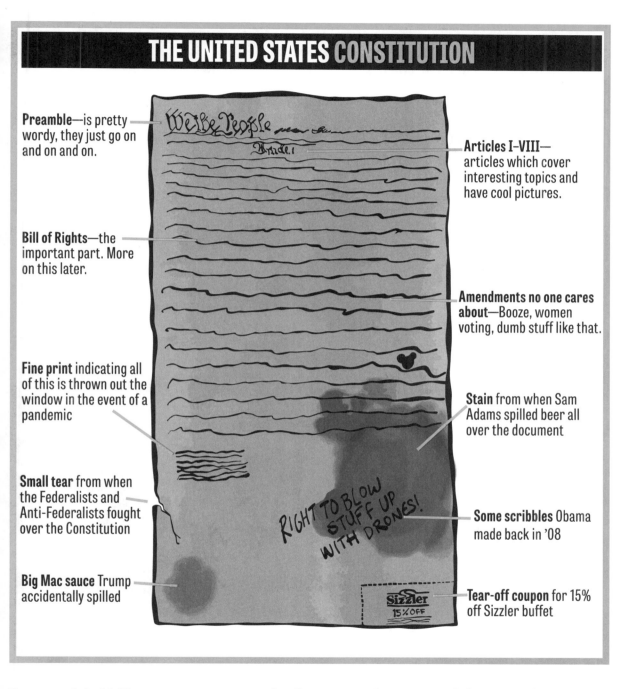

Pretty cool, huh? For over two centuries, the Constitution has protected American freedom, and now we have all this cool stuff like airplanes, space stations, video games, scented candles, dog spas, and pizza! Wow! What a great country!

But as it was at our founding, freedom is always under attack from dark foreign and domestic forces, whether by British redcoats firing cannons at your face or pink-haired Communists trying to teach your 5-year-old that freedom is bad, or most likely, **our own government**.

If we are to protect our freedom and Consitution from its enemies, it's important to know our rights and be ready to defend them with our lives. Or, at least, know what to be mad about when the government takes them away.

Here is a handy list of your constitutional rights, broken down in layman's terms:

THE CONSTITUTION: THE BILL OF RIGHTS

1ST AMENDMENT

The freedom of speech: You can say anything you want! Unless you're yelling "fire" in a crowded theater. Or using social media. Or you don't want to lose your job. Or you're on a college campus. Or your speech is really, really hateful. Or just kinda distasteful. Or you want to burn a flag. Other than that, free speech!

2ND AMENDMENT

The right to bear arms: not sure what the Founders were thinking here. Guns? For EVERYONE??! At least it only applies to flintlock muskets. And only after a long background check. And taking a class. And filling out a form. And paying $600. Other than that, this right is unalienable.

3RD AMENDMENT

Soldiers aren't allowed to use your home without your permission, forcing them to sleep outside in tents all the time. Cruel!

4TH AMENDMENT

No unreasonable search and seizure: The government isn't allowed to perform an unreasonable search of your private property. Unless they think you have weed or something. In that case, they're allowed to bash your door down at 3 a.m. and shoot you in your bed.

5TH AMENDMENT

You have the right not to testify against yourself, not be held indefinitely without charges, and you have the right not to go on *Double Jeopardy!* You are still subject to regular *Jeopardy!* and *Final Jeopardy!*, however.

6TH AMENDMENT

Trial by jury: You have the right to a trial by twelve angry men who are all really mad that they couldn't get out of jury duty and have to sit there for weeks while you go on and on maintaining your innocence.

SEVERAL YEARS LATER

7TH AMENDMENT

You have the right to a fair and speedy trial. This means you cannot be waiting around for your day in court as long as you would at the DMV.

8TH AMENDMENT

No cruel or unusual punishment. This means you cannot be punished by having a mask forced over your head while cultists pour bees in. NOT THE BEES! NOT THE BEES!

9TH AMENDMENT

Non-enumerated rights: turns out you have more rights than just the ones in the Constitution, but the Founders got bored and didn't write them all down. Like you have the right to scarf down Cheetos, dance like no one is watching, or give an AR-15 to a bear.

10TH AMENDMENT

Powers not given to the federal government or denied by the Consitution are retained by the people and the states. Awesome states like Texas. Mmm, Texas. Yup.

THE CONSTITUTION: MORE AMENDMENTS

11th Amendment
You can sue an entire state! Cool!

12th Amendment
Election of a president and vice president:
Washington refused to be King of America, so
we decided to go with calling them presidents
and just treat them like kings instead.

13th Amendment
Abolition of slavery: Now we're talking! This
should have been a given, considering the
Preamble and Bill of Rights, but Democrats
never liked the Bill of Rights anyway.

14th Amendment
Citizens cannot be deprived of life, liberty, or
property without due process: Unborn babies
need not apply.

15th Amendment
Guaranteed voting rights regardless of race or
previous slave status: Democrats, for goodness
sakes, give it up already. You lost!

16th Amendment
Created the federal income tax: The darkest day
in American history

17th Amendment
Senators now elected by popular vote rather
than appointed by representatives: This change
did little to improve the cesspool of corruption
that is the Senate.

18th Amendment
Prohibited alcohol: Those darn Baptists and
their shenanigans!

19th Amendment
Women given the right to vote: Historians
believe this is when everything started going
downhill.

20th Amendment
Established the presidential line of succession:
Say hello to President Kamala Harris!

21st Amendment
Repealed alcohol prohibition: After over a decade
of bad moonshine and Tommy gun drive-bys,
the Irish Catholics finally prevailed over the
Baptists and brought back alcohol! Rejoice!

22nd Amendment
Limited the president to serving only two terms:
This can only be overturned if the president
enters the Konami Code to grant himself
infinite terms.

23rd Amendment
Residents of D.C. can vote for president now?
These amendments keep getting worse.

24th Amendment
Abolition of the poll tax: This was long seen as
an effective means of preventing the scourge of
women voting, but no more!

25th Amendment
Process for removing an incapacitated or
mentally unfit president, like the one currently
serving.

26th Amendment
Right to vote starting at age 18:
NOOOOOOOOOOOOOOO!

27th Amendment
Congress can't vote themselves pay raises that
take effect during the course of a session: Nice!
Congress got around this by implementing
automatic pay raises to kick in every
four years. Boo.

LESSER-KNOWN RIGHTS

Did you know that you have other rights that aren't spelled out in the first ten amendments? Know your rights so you can defend them:

The right to own an awesome M1 Abrams tank

The right to free healthcare

The right to free internet

The right to unlimited breadsticks

The right to an awesome attorney, like Lionel Hutz from *The Simpsons*

The right to a gay-trans polygamous marriage to a tree

The right to remain awesome

The right to binge-watch all of *The Mandalorian* in one sitting

The right to murder your unborn baby for any reason whatsoever

INTERPRETING THE CONSTITUTION

Since the Constitution is unclear and written in an extraterrestrial runic language, it's important to have interpreters to help us know what it really means. These interpretations will vary depending on whether you're on the Right or the Left.

Conservative interpretation

The words of the Constitution are etched in stone by the hand of God Himself. It is without error or fault in all of its teachings, infallible in all its original writings. It is designed to limit the power of tyrants and bureaucrats to force COVID masks and gayness on us.

Amen.

Leftist interpretation

The Constitution is a living, breathing document that can only be interpreted by divine mystic sages with big, caring hearts. It was originally written by mean racists who wanted to limit the power of the loving, caring, and generous federal government. Over time, it has evolved into a magical blank check that lets us do whatever we want as long as we can get the right people in power. This is for your own good.

CONSERVATIVES

Etched in stone, by God Himself

Without error or fault

Limits power of tyrants and bureaucrats

Repels COVID and gayness

Should be enshrined in holy temple

Read it as morning devotional

LEFTISTS

Living, breathing, ever-changing

Requires smart people with Rosetta Stones to interpret the true meaning

Has racist roots, and is anti-government

Produces unlimited funds

Run over it with an industrial forklift

Steal it from Archives and launch it into space

HOW TO INTERPRET THE CONSTITUTION

STEP 1: LAY OUT YOUR POLITICAL AGENDA

STEP 2: BEND THE HECK OUT OF THE CONSTITUTION TO SUIT YOUR AGENDA'S NEEDS

STEP 3: CONGRATULATIONS! THE CONSTITUTION NOW SUPPORTS YOUR AGENDA!

THE RIGHT TO BEAR ARMS:
THE FREEDOM THAT GUARANTEES ALL OTHERS

The 2nd Amendment, which guarantees the right to bear arms, is the most awesome of all the rights. Unlike places like Britain, Australia, and North Korea, you can own firearms here in America.

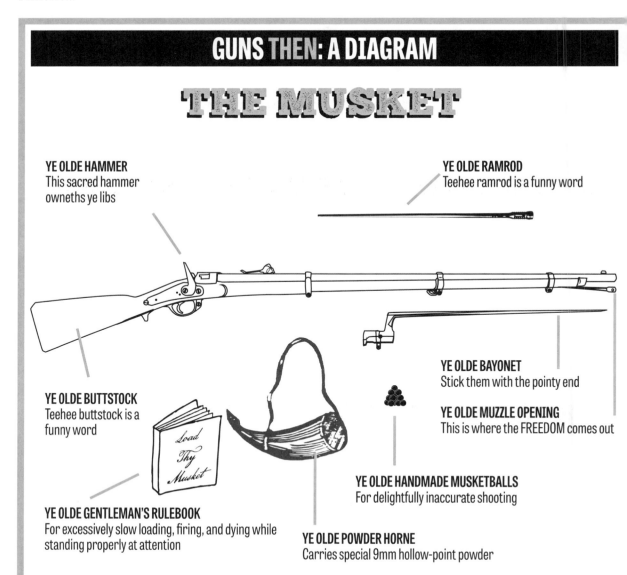

GUNS THEN: A DIAGRAM

THE MUSKET

YE OLDE HAMMER
This sacred hammer owneths ye libs

YE OLDE RAMROD
Teehee ramrod is a funny word

YE OLDE BUTTSTOCK
Teehee buttstock is a funny word

YE OLDE BAYONET
Stick them with the pointy end

YE OLDE MUZZLE OPENING
This is where the FREEDOM comes out

YE OLDE GENTLEMAN'S RULEBOOK
For excessively slow loading, firing, and dying while standing properly at attention

YE OLDE HANDMADE MUSKETBALLS
For delightfully inaccurate shooting

YE OLDE POWDER HORNE
Carries special 9mm hollow-point powder

Load Thy Musket

Firearms are what protect us from government overreach and tyranny. In the olden days, the government could send soldiers armed with muskets to your home, but they can't do that now since we have guns to protect ourselves. Instead, now they just send three militarized SWAT divisions in tanks and a couple helicopters to arrest you. Freedom!

Guns have changed over the years, and many people debate whether people should be allowed to have scary-looking semi-automatic firearms when only muskets existed when the 2nd Amendment was written.

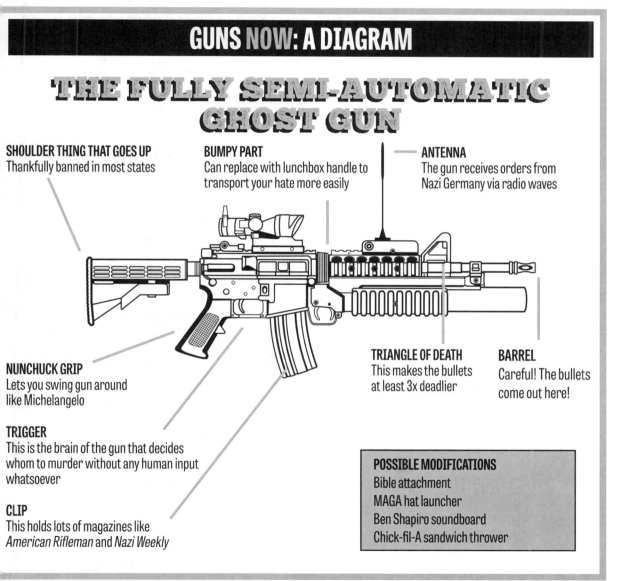

GUNS NOW: A DIAGRAM

THE FULLY SEMI-AUTOMATIC GHOST GUN

SHOULDER THING THAT GOES UP
Thankfully banned in most states

BUMPY PART
Can replace with lunchbox handle to transport your hate more easily

ANTENNA
The gun receives orders from Nazi Germany via radio waves

NUNCHUCK GRIP
Lets you swing gun around like Michelangelo

TRIGGER
This is the brain of the gun that decides whom to murder without any human input whatsoever

CLIP
This holds lots of magazines like *American Rifleman* and *Nazi Weekly*

TRIANGLE OF DEATH
This makes the bullets at least 3x deadlier

BARREL
Careful! The bullets come out here!

POSSIBLE MODIFICATIONS
Bible attachment
MAGA hat launcher
Ben Shapiro soundboard
Chick-fil-A sandwich thrower

Since our firearms have grown in sheer evil deadliness over the years, the government has had to increase its firepower as well. To make sure private citizens don't have too much power, they're only allowed to own certain weapons. We still long for the days of choices. Choices and selections. Choices of directions, and choices that can add a little freedom in your life. Here's a handy guide to keep you out of trouble:

HANDY DANDY WEAPON OWNERSHIP GUIDE

WEAPONS YOU CAN OWN	WEAPONS THE GOVERNMENT CAN OWN
AR-15	MACHINE GUNS
PISTOL	TANKS
FANCY COWBOY REVOLVER	STEALTH FIGHTERS
LADY-SIZED DERRINGER	DRONES
SLINGSHOT	NUKES
NUNCHUCKS	BATTLESHIPS
BOW AND ARROW	JEWISH SPACE LASERS
SAMURAI SWORD	ALIEN WEAPON TECHNOLOGY FROM PLANET CYBERTRON
ELON MUSK'S FLAMETHROWER	TRANSGENDER ADMIRALS
MEAN TWEETS	KAMALA HARRIS'S LAUGH
UNMASKED FACES THAT COULD SPREAD COVID	TAX AUDITS
FISTS	FAKE FBI PIPE BOMBS
BANANA PEELS	WINGED BLUE SPINY SHELL

HOW TO EXERCISE YOUR CONSTITUTIONAL RIGHTS

What good are rights if you don't use 'em? If you're an American, it's essential that you proudly and boldly exercise your rights. Here's how to do it:

Burn an American Flag

There's no better way to show your pride in your American right to free speech.

Buy a Machine Gun and Fire It into the Air

You can go do that right now, as it's your God-given right. Unless you live in California.

Use Flagrant Hate Speech Online

Call someone a marshmallow-filled buffoon. The feds can't stop you. Though Twitter might ban you.

Buy Moonshine from a Bootlegger

Go find a shack in Kentucky, slide $5 under the door, and tell them Jim-Bob sent you. Good stuff.

Commit a Crime and Get Tried by a Jury
You'll never appreciate your rights until you do.

Kill a Person
So you can get punished in a non-cruel, non-unusual way.

Quarter Soldiers in Your Home
. . . but of your own free will

Screech Loudly in Your Political Opponents' Faces
As long as you don't touch them, you can scream whatever you want. Fun!

Aren't you thankful we have a Constitution that protects our rights, and a bunch of guns just in case that doesn't work?

The Constitution is a work of genius that protects our unalienable right to be free. It protects us from the tyranny of the majority and restrains the government from overreach. As long as we all continue to keep obeying it. Yikes—sounds as if this whole freedom thing is very fragile and depends on us to keep it alive!

Get a little freedom in your life, and good luck keeping it alive!

CHAPTER REVIEW: KNOW YOUR CONSTITUTIONAL RIGHTS

We've discussed so many incredible things in these last few pages. Let's take a minute to check our comprehension for absolutely no reason whatsoever.

1. Which one of these amendments personally spoke to your heart? Why?

2. How many guns do you own and what is the combination to your safe?

3. Have you ever used hate speech? What did you say? Say it again now, we dare you.

4. James Madison wrote that "the powers delegated by the proposed Constitution to the federal government are few and defined. Those which are to remain in the State governments are numerous and indefinite." Lysander Spooner later wrote, "But whether the Constitution really be one thing, or another, this much is certain—that it has either authorized such a government as we have had, or has been powerless to prevent it. In either case, it is unfit to exist." In the space provided, please evaluate the health of this living, breathing Constitution in the twenty-first century.

5. Do you know any eighteen-year-olds? If so, have you asked them to please not vote?

6. OK, I can't stop thinking about it. Did you ACTUALLY touch the gavel in Chapter 5?

Chapter 8

Winning (and Rigging) Elections

Now we come to the heart and soul of democracy: **ELECTIONS!** Elections are fun because we all get to vote on who runs our country for the next several years. You get to pick a side and cheer for them and boo the other side. You get to feel happy when your side wins, as the country is saved, and you get to feel angry when the other side wins, because now we're all screwed and the country is going down the crapper.

It's a winner-takes-all, no-holds-barred DEATHMATCH for the fate of the country,

SUNDAY, SUNDAY, **SUNDAY**!

But, perhaps most importantly, elections can be *rigged*. Rather than nominating good candidates and listening to the needs of the people, you can simply manipulate things like a puppet master to ensure that you and your party stay in power *forever*.

Doesn't that sound great?

Of course it does.

Being in power is awesome. Being in power never has any negative side effects whatsoever.

Think about Frodo in *Lord of the Rings*. He got to hold the Ring of Power. And that turned him invisible. And he ended up saving the world. All of that because of his relentless pursuit of power. And there weren't any negative consequences of wielding that much power. It's a win-win.

But how exactly is the sausage made? Mmm, sausage.

We gotta stop writing this book while we're hungry.

Anyway, buckle in as we take you on a tour of the important process of voting, elections, and the rigging that makes it all possible.

PRO TIP

IF YOU EVER FIND A RING OF POWER, KEEP IT FOREVER

We wants it. My Precious.

DID YOU KNOW?

Experts have found that every election you participate in is the most important election in the history of the universe and that if your side loses, it is the end of democracy as we know it.

PRESIDENTIAL ELECTIONS: FIGHT! FIGHT! FIGHT!

THE PATH TO UNLIMITED COSMIC POLITICAL POWER

START

BIRTHPLACE	MINIMUM AGE	US RESIDENCY
USA	**35**	**14**
* PREFERABLY AN OLD WHITE MAN	* THEN DOUBLE IT	YEARS

PREREQUISITES

STEP 4: DEBATES

There are several presidential debates, which are often confused with a broadcast from an old folks' home where two old white men are shouting incoherently at each other.

R   D

STEP 5: THE MOMENT OF TRUTH

Finally, on the first Tuesday of November, people come from far and wide to cast their votes.
News media freaks out.
Population freaks out.
ERRYBODY GONNA FREAK OUT!!!

Polls close at 8 p.m., but counting will not be finished until Democrats get the results they want.

STEP 6: ELECTORAL COLLEGE

After each state's vote tally is certified, electors are selected for the winning candidate. They all go vote in Washington, D.C., which always goes smoothly.

Well, **ALMOST** always.

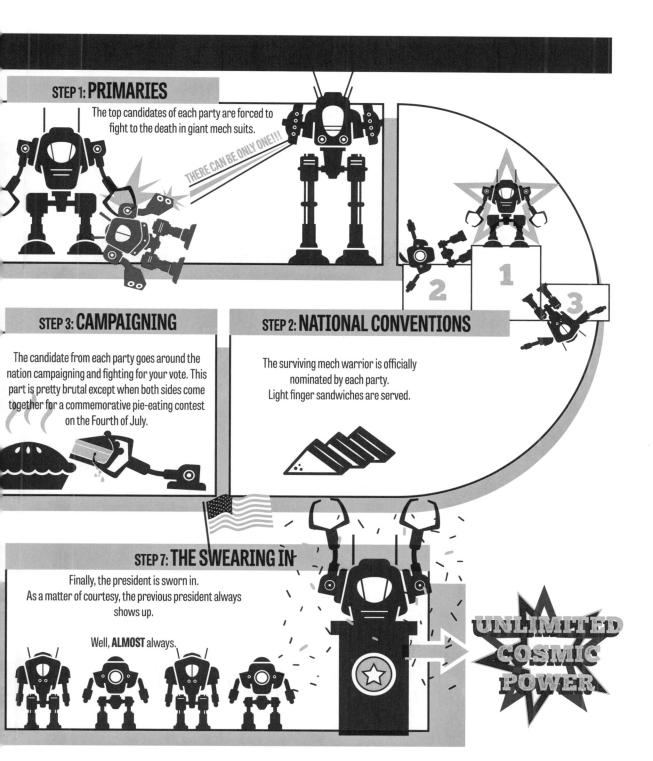

STEP 1: PRIMARIES

The top candidates of each party are forced to fight to the death in giant mech suits.

THERE CAN BE ONLY ONE!!!

STEP 3: CAMPAIGNING

The candidate from each party goes around the nation campaigning and fighting for your vote. This part is pretty brutal except when both sides come together for a commemorative pie-eating contest on the Fourth of July.

STEP 2: NATIONAL CONVENTIONS

The surviving mech warrior is officially nominated by each party.
Light finger sandwiches are served.

STEP 7: THE SWEARING IN

Finally, the president is sworn in.
As a matter of courtesy, the previous president always shows up.

Well, **ALMOST** always.

UNLIMITED COSMIC POWER

ELECTIONS AND YOU

Does this all seem super confusing?

Don't worry, you don't need to pay a ton of attention during the primaries. Everyone and their mom throws their hat in the ring during the primaries. But the Deep State lizard cabal has already picked the people they want to win, so you can just sit back and enjoy the show.

However, once the general election starts, you can't help but get drawn in. You're going to be inundated with political ads from both sides of the aisle. Buckle up, because you're going to be seeing TONS of these.

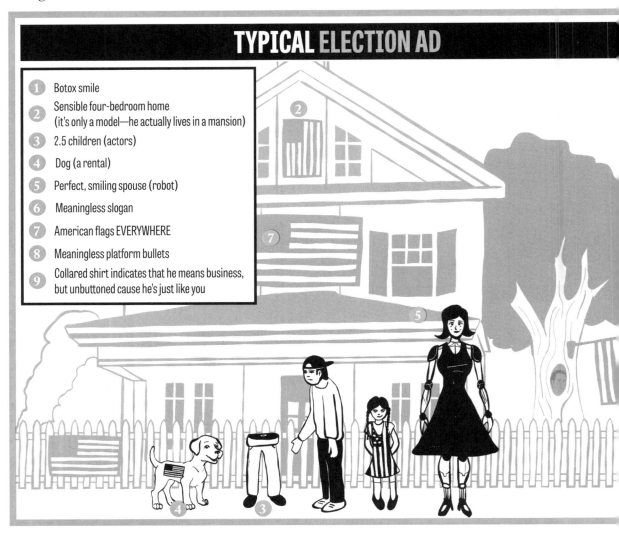

TYPICAL ELECTION AD

1. Botox smile
2. Sensible four-bedroom home (it's only a model—he actually lives in a mansion)
3. 2.5 children (actors)
4. Dog (a rental)
5. Perfect, smiling spouse (robot)
6. Meaningless slogan
7. American flags EVERYWHERE
8. Meaningless platform bullets
9. Collared shirt indicates that he means business, but unbuttoned cause he's just like you

Every street corner you drive by will have the names of several criminals pasted on the fence for some reason.

The important thing to remember about all these ads is not a single word of them is true. They are for entertainment purposes only.

SLING SOME MUD

Of course, politicians don't just lie to make themselves look good. You've got to make your opponent look bad! This is a good, old-fashioned democratic tradition called mudslinging, and it's where you dig up old tweets, bad opinions, or risque stuff your opponent did (allegedly) and drop the news at the most advantageous time possible.

MUD GENERATOR

Using this handy generator, you can come up with some GOOD MUD to sling at your opponent:

For each column, roll a twelve-sided die (not included with this book; go buy a copy of the *Dungeons & Dragons* starter kit), and the result will indicate which labels you should apply to your opponent. If you're a noob, you can use two normie-dice, but you'll never roll a 1.

A	B	C	D
1. Sickly	1. Scum-sucking	1. Racist	1. Cheesebag
2. No-good	2. Puppy-hating	2. Pony	2. Juggalo
3. One-eyed	3. Dog-faced	3. Sexist	3. Square
4. Slimy	4. Yellow-bellied	4. Nazi	4. Poo-poo head
5. Lyin'	5. Commie-lovin'	5. Vegan	5. Soldier
6. Philanderin'	6. Gun-totin'	6. Crossfitting	6. Socialist
7. Cheatin'	7. Cake-chowin'	7. Misogynist	7. Guy Named Steve
8. Highfalutin	8. Half-cocked	8. Sizzly	8. Yokel
9. Sizzlin'	9. Four-eyed	9. Ageist	9. Papist
10. Woke	10. Slack-jawed	10. Italian	10. Calvinist
11. Yammerin'	11. Sizzler-eatin'	11. Egalitarian	11. Sizzler Manager
12. Posticulatin'	12. Molasses-brained	12. Greasy	12. Dumpster Hammock

For instance, depending on your results, you might call your opponent a **sickly Commie-lovin' Nazi juggalo**. That's pretty brutal. Nobody wants to be called a juggalo, after all. Or, it could be a more outlandish, unrealistic result, like **lyin' dog-faced pony soldier**.

But that insult would probably never be used in real life.

Sickly Commie-Lovin' Nazi Juggalo

Lyin' Dog-Faced Pony Soldier

Or, come up with your own insults. The sky's the limit. Be creative! The important thing is that you impugn your opponent's character for your own political advancement.

Everybody wins.

Except your opponent.

And probably America.

THE UNION CIRCUIT

Money plays a large part in getting politicians elected. One of the primary sources of money comes from public sector union donations. In 2020, 89 percent of public sector unions donations went to elect Democrat politicians.

HERE'S HOW IT WORKS:

The elected legislator uses your taxpayer dollars to set the pay scale of the public sector employees who must pay the public sector unions who pay the politicians who set the pay scale of the public sector employees who must pay the public sector unions who pay the politicians who set the pay scale of the public sector employees who must pay the public sector unions who pay the politicians who set the pay scale of the public sector employees who must pay the public sector unions who pay the politicians who set set the pay scale of the public sector employees who must pay the public sector unions who pay the politicians who set the pay scale of the public sector employees who must pay the public sector unions who pay the politicians who set the pay scale of the public sector employees who must pay the public sector unions who pay the politicians who set the pay scale of the public sector employees who must pay the public sector unions who pay the politicians who set the pay scale of the public sector employees who must pay the public sector unions who pay the politicians who set the pay scale of the public sector employees who must pay the public sector unions who pay the politicians who set the pay scale of the public sector employees who must pay the public sector unions who pay the politicians who set the pay scale of the public sector employees who must pay the public sector unions who pay the politicians who set the pay scale of the public sector employees who must pay the public sector unions who pay the politicians who set the pay scale of the public sector employees who must pay the public sector unions who pay the politicians who set the pay scale of the public sector employees who must pay the public sector unions who pay the politicians who set the pay scale of the public sector employees who must pay the public sector unions who pay the politicians who set the pay scale of the public sector employees who must pay the public sector unions who pay the politicians who set the pay scale of the public sector employees who must pay the public sector unions who pay the politicians who set the pay scale of the public sector employees who must pay the public sector unions who pay the politicians who set the pay scale of the public sector employees who must pay the public sector unions who pay the politicians who set the pay scale of the public sector employees who must pay the public sector unions who pay the politicians who set the pay scale of the public sector employees who must pay the public sector unions who pay the politicians who set the pay scale of the public sector employees who must pay the public sector unions who pay the politicians who set the pay scale of the public sector employees who must pay the public sector unions who pay the politicians who set the pay scale of the public sector employees who must pay the public sector unions who pay the politicians who set the pay scale of the public sector employees who must pay the public sector unions who pay the politicians who set the pay scale of the public sector employees who must pay the public sector unions who pay the politicians who set the pay scale of the public sector employees who must pay the public sector unions who pay the politicians who set the pay scale of the public sector employees who must pay the public sector unions who pay the politicians who set the pay scale of the public sector employees who must pay the public sector unions who pay the politicians who set the pay scale of the public sector employees who must pay the public sector unions who pay the politicians who set the pay scale of the public sector employees who must pay the public sector unions who pay the politicians who set the pay scale of the public sector employees who must pay the public sector unions who pay the politicians who set the pay scale of the public sector employees who must pay the public sector unions who pay the politicians who set the pay scale of the public sector employees who must pay the public sector unions who pay the politicians who set the pay scale of the public sector employees who must pay the public sector unions who pay the politicians who set the pay scale of the public sector employees who must pay the public sector unions who pay the politicians who set the pay scale of the public sector employees who must pay the public sector unions who pay the politicians who set the pay scale of the public sector employees who must pay the public sector unions who pay the politicians who set the pay scale of the public sector employees who must pay the public sector unions who pay the politicians who set the pay scale of the public sector employees who must pay the public sector unions who pay the politicians who set the pay scale of the public sector employees who must pay the public sector unions who pay the politicians who set the pay scale of the public sector employees who must pay the public sector unions who pay the politicians who set the pay scale of the public sector employees who must pay the public sector unions who pay the politicians who set the pay scale of the public sector employees who must pay the public sector unions who pay the politicians who set the pay scale of the public sector employees who must pay the public sector unions who pay the politicians who...

Make sense? Great!

THE ELECTORAL COLLEGE

In a presidential election, we don't vote for president directly. Instead, each state votes for **electors**, who then cast their vote for president.

The candidate who gets the most electoral votes is the winner, which means the candidate who wins the popular vote may not even win the election. This is fun because then they can scream and cry about how unfair that is for at least four years.

The important thing to remember about the Electoral College is that it is racist and anti-democratic, unless your side wins the election. Then it is fair and balanced and the last bastion of true democracy in the world.

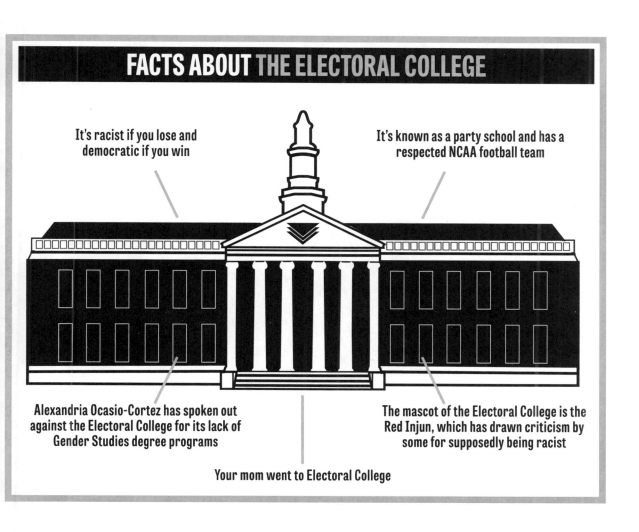

FACTS ABOUT THE ELECTORAL COLLEGE

It's racist if you lose and democratic if you win

It's known as a party school and has a respected NCAA football team

Alexandria Ocasio-Cortez has spoken out against the Electoral College for its lack of Gender Studies degree programs

The mascot of the Electoral College is the Red Injun, which has drawn criticism by some for supposedly being racist

Your mom went to Electoral College

Politicians will need to know where to focus their efforts when it comes to campaigning.

Here's a handy map of every state—well, every state that matters, anyway, when it comes to winning elections and the electoral vote count for each:

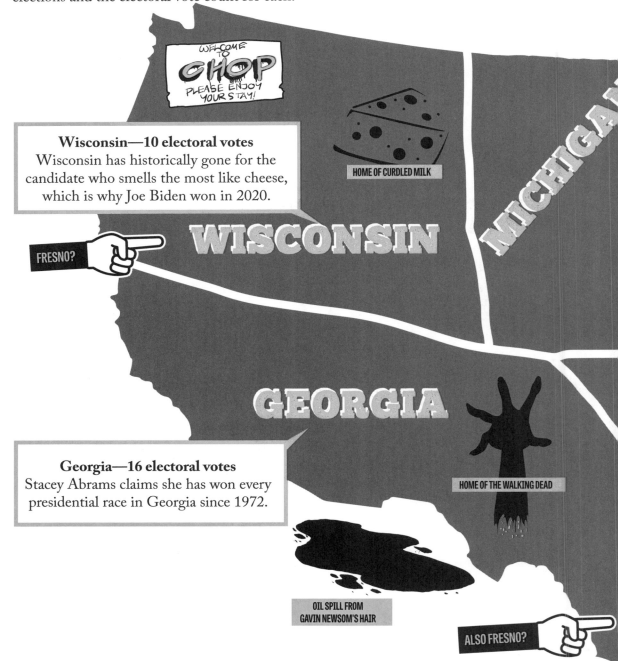

Wisconsin—10 electoral votes
Wisconsin has historically gone for the candidate who smells the most like cheese, which is why Joe Biden won in 2020.

Georgia—16 electoral votes
Stacey Abrams claims she has won every presidential race in Georgia since 1972.

THE ELECTORAL MAP

CANADA?

Michigan—15 electoral votes
All fifteen of Michigan's electoral votes are counted in the middle of the night without supervision to ensure maximum fairness.

AMERICA'S GLOVE

Pennsylvania—19 electoral votes
The fact that it's a swing state is the most interesting thing about Pennsylvania.

PENNSYLVANIA

HOME OF FAMED STREET RAPPER B-RABBIT

HOME OF ROCKY BALBOA

HI, I'M IN... DELAWARE

FLORIDA

THE HALLOWED LOCATION WHERE IN 1998, THE UNDERTAKER THREW MANKIND OFF HELL IN A CELL, AND PLUMMETED 16FT THROUGH AN ANNOUNCER'S TABLE.

OLD PEOPLE

Florida—30 electoral votes
The winner of every presidential race in Florida has to claim his thirty votes by walking a tightrope across a crocodile pond. It's a beloved tradition.

FINAL RESTING PLACE OF HILLARY CLINTON'S EMAILS

AMERICA'S UDDERS

RIGGING AN ELECTION

You could always try to win an election fair and square, but that's not very fun. :(

Instead, try rigging an election so that you can win every time. It's a win-win situation. Well, not for the loser. But it is for you and your political party, which is all that's really important.

Campaign at the local cemetery

You've gotta get the word out.

Switch to voting by carrier pigeon

It's safe and secure.

Get Twitter to ban all the bad news about your candidate

You don't even have to rig the election yourself—you can let Big Tech do it!

Have Russian hackers post some memes

A few memes on Facebook oughta do it.

RIGGING AN ELECTION (CONTINUED)

Sneak three people into polling place

By stacking them on top of each other in a trenchcoat.

Release bees in polling place

Yes, the bees! Yes, THE BEES!!!

Lower through roof of ballot-counting location

Like in *Mission Impossible*, and steal ballots.

Claim a pipe burst

As the ballots were being counted. Oh well, whatcha gonna do?

RIGGING AN ELECTION (CONTINUED)

Add hundreds of thousands of votes

To your candidate in the middle of the night. No one will notice.

Invent a virus in a lab

To overthrow the president.

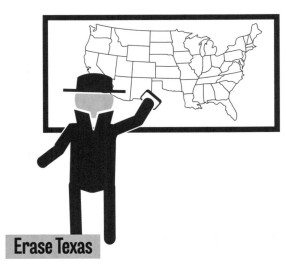

Erase Texas

From all maps in the nation. Muahahaha!

Harvest votes

With industrial-sized vote harvester.

But the most important thing to remember about election meddling is that if you win, it was the **fairest election in the history of the world**. If your side loses, it was the **most rigged and unfair election ever held in the history of the universe**.

Just take a look at this handy chart:

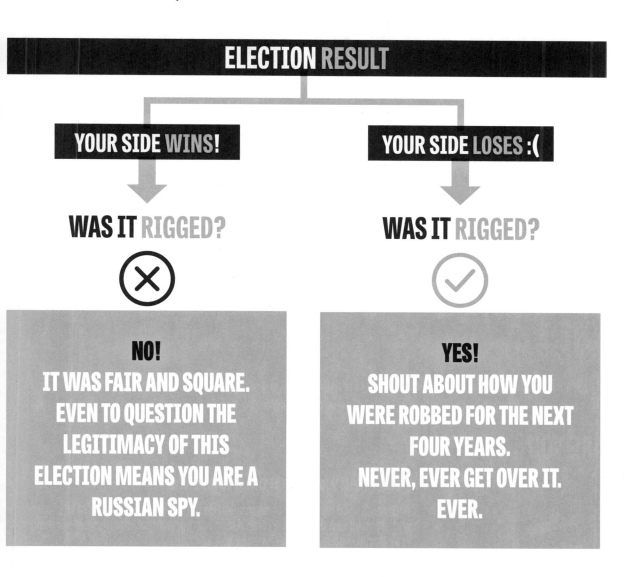

VOTER SUPPRESSION

Have you experienced voter suppression? Dozens suffer every year. Look for these key indicators of voter suppression:

SIGNS YOU MIGHT BE SURPRESSED

- You have to wait in line.
- You are asked to show your ID.
- You are told you have to make it through a hedge maze to get to the ballot booth.
- The polling place is guarded by Dwayne "The Rock" Johnson.
- To drop off your ballot you must jump over those giant spinning fireball arms like in Bowser's castle.
- The poll attendant says, "Have a nice day."
- You are denied the right to vote despite the fact that you are an undead zombie.
- The poll worker is trying to keep you away by playing "Kokomo" by The Beach Boys at full blast.
- The polling place is not giving away free beer.
- You are a Democrat.

Russia has been known to meddle in our elections from time to time. In fact, you might be a Russian spy and not even realize it. Check for these signs to see if you are actually a Russian spy:

ARE YOU A RUSSIAN SPY?

You often wake up from a fugue state.

With fractured memories of swimming deep under the icy waves of the Atlantic and planting explosive devices on American nuclear submarines before making your harrowing escape on the back of a sea lion.

This is a pretty significant tell. You're definitely some kind of sleeper agent!

You love the color red.

Your bed sheets are red. Your favorite shirt is red. Even the great, honorable hammer-and-sickle flag of the Soviet Union that flies out in front of your house is red.

These are all signs that you are definitely a Russian spy—better flee the country before you are outed by CNN!

You're constantly running into Vladimir Putin.

Sure, we've all bumped into the Russian president now and again. But if you run into him once too often—while grabbing your morning coffee, as you board the subway, while you're being debriefed from a classified mission in which you hacked into government mainframes to influence the election in favor of Trump—there's a slight chance you could be an intelligence agent in service of the Kremlin.

You occasionally find yourself uncontrollably screaming, "WORKERS OF THE WORLD, UNITE!"

This is often one of the most common signs that you're a brainwashed Russian robot and have been for decades, and you're ready to be activated at a moment's notice to do Putin's dirty work and meddle in U.S. affairs. You may yell this slogan in the middle of the night, while you're ordering okroshka at your favorite ethnic restaurant, or as you infiltrate a top-secret U.S. military installation in order to sabotage the capitalist pigs' nuclear weapons.

You sometimes approved of President Trump's policies.

If you have the slightest feelings of admiration for The Donald, or even occasionally approve of one of his policies even if you're not a big fan of the man himself, there's a very good chance you have ties to Russia. Studies show that almost 97 percent of U.S. citizens who voted against Hillary Clinton in the 2016 election were actually rogue sleeper agents taking orders directly from Moscow.

GO FORTH AND RIG ELECTIONS

Well, now you know literally everything there is to know about elections. So now you can go forth and participate in the political process!

But what happens if you don't get your way, you might be asking?

Great question. How'd you get so smart, Steve? That's another beautiful part of our democracy: holding insurrections and peaceful protests. Read on, my friend, to learn how to cry and scream when you don't get your way.

CHAPTER REVIEW: WINNING (AND RIGGING) ELECTIONS

We've discussed so many incredible things in these last few pages. Let's take a minute to check our comprehension for absolutely no reason whatsoever.

1. What is the election in your life that you need to focus on?

2. Do you know anyone who voted for Ralph Nader? Have you ever punched them? Why or why not?

3. Are you a Russian spy? This is for posterity, so, please—be honest.

4. ARE YOU A RUSSIAN SPY?! TALK, COMMIE!

5. John Adams said, "Remember, democracy never lasts long. It soon wastes, exhausts, and murders itself. There is never a democracy that did not commit suicide." Alexander Hamilton seemed to agree by stating, "Real liberty is neither found in despotism or the extremes of democracy, but in moderate governments." In the space provided, please explain how the Founding Fathers got it wrong in establishing an Electoral College rather than a direct democratic election for deciding who shall be the president.

6. Why don't you just get your own gavel?

Chapter 9

Insurrections and (Mostly) Peaceful Protests

So, you've tried to win an election, but you've lost. You can't just lie down, roll over, and accept the fact that you'll have to get along without getting your way for a while. You can't just compromise with the other side and do your best to win next time.

NEVER!

It's time to take drastic measures.

SO YOU'VE JUST LOST AN ELECTION

Civil unrest often leads to people assembling in protest.

Depending on whether you're on the Left or the Right, this means you need to participate in one of two different staples of democracy: an **insurrection** or a **mostly peaceful protest**.

If you're a conservative, it's time for an insurrection. This means you impotently storm the Capitol, take some selfies, and call it a day. It's mostly like an Xtreme tour of the Capitol Building, with the added bonus that you get to spend an indefinite amount of time in federal prison for it.

If you're a liberal, it's time for a mostly peaceful protest. This means you burn down absolutely everything in sight, especially minority-owned businesses, and you get applauded in the media for it. You might even get nominated for a Nobel Peace Prize.

Mr. Bob Peace
INVENTOR OF THE NOBEL PEACE PRIZE

HOW TO TELL AN INSURRECTION FROM A PEACEFUL PROTEST

If you stumble across a group of agitated people gathered at the Capitol, a federal courthouse, or other political location, how do you know if it's an insurrection or a peaceful protest?

Consult this handy chart for the telltale signs of each:

INSURRECTION	PEACEFUL PROTEST
ANGRY PEOPLE WEARING MAGA HATS	ANGRY PEOPLE WEARING CHE GUEVARA SHIRTS
LITTLE DESTRUCTION OF PROPERTY	BURN EVERYTHING IN SIGHT
COPS POLITELY LET THEM IN	COPS TRY TO STOP THEM BUT GET BRICKED
TAKE SELFIES	BEAT YOU TO DEATH WITH SELFIE STICK
LEADERS SPECIFICALLY SAY, "STAY PEACEFUL"	LEADERS SPECIFICALLY SAY, "DEATH TO COPS"
PROTESTS AT GOVERNMENT BUILDING	PROTESTS ANYWHERE THERE ARE EXPENSIVE NIKES
CONDEMNED BY MEDIA	PRAISED BY MEDIA
AT LEAST ONE COOL BUFFALO COSTUME	ZERO COOL BUFFALO COSTUMES
IMPRISONED INDEFINITELY	KAMALA HARRIS BAILS OUT IMMEDIATELY

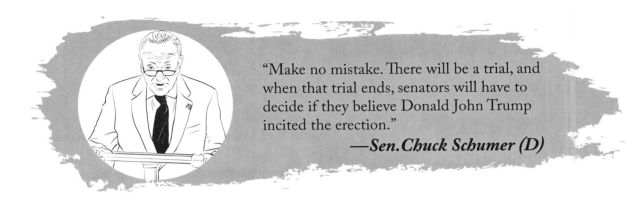

"Make no mistake. There will be a trial, and when that trial ends, senators will have to decide if they believe Donald John Trump incited the erection."

—*Sen. Chuck Schumer (D)*

JANUARY 6: A DAY THAT WILL LIVE IN INFAMY

Just in case you haven't tuned into CNN for the last year or so (which, let's be honest, is pretty likely unless you've been in a lot of airports or hotel lobbies), it's time to tell you about January 6, 2021. On that fateful day, hundreds, perhaps thousands, of Trump supporters stormed the U.S. Capitol Building, breaking through the barriers the cops erected but then politely moved aside for them.

Their mission succeeded, and they managed to take selfies, steal a podium, and claim the country in the name of Buffalo Man in the process.

It was a horrible day. It was worse than 9/11, the sinking of the *Titanic*, and the release of the female *Ghostbusters* reboot all combined.

Wow. That's pretty bad.

Let's take a moment to remember all those people killed by Trump supporters on that horrible day.

Please look at the next page, remove your hat, and observe a moment of silence.

HOW TO CONDUCT AN INSURRECTION

If you're on the right and you lose an election, you might choose to stage an insurrection. Let's look at some handy tips for throwing an awesome insurrection:

Climb Capitol wall like Mario in *Donkey Kong*

Daaah dah dah dah DAAAAAAH DAH!

Dress like Hamburglar and steal Nancy Pelosi's podium

Can't catch me, Ronald! Hahaha!

Deploy Mike Pence-seeking robot murder hornets

They can sense marital faithfulness and personal integrity.

Ride in on buffalo and claim rightful place on throne

He's a guy on a buffalooooo!

Have everyone dress up like Trump

They won't know which one is the real Trump. They can't arrest all of you.

Use *Portal* gun to drop giant anvil on Capitol Building

It was a triumph . . .

Use catapult to launch Trump over wall to his rightful place as ruler

At dawn, look to the east!

Elbow-drop Capitol police from top rope

WITH GOD AS MY WITNESS HE IS BROKEN IN HALF!

HOW TO CONDUCT A PEACEFUL PROTEST

If you're on the left and you think the president is a deranged orange Nazi, you might instead choose to hold a peaceful protest. Let's look at some tips for pulling that off:

Punch a cop to promote tolerance

LOVE! TOLERANCE! KAPOW!

Use flamethrower on minority-owned businesses

Feel the heat of my love for you!

Shout, "For racial equity!" while stealing Nikes

It cancels out the crime.

Bring forklift for your massive TV haul

Only if you are a certified forklift operator.

Deploy Andy Ngo-seeking robot murder hornets

They sense actual journalism and gayness.

Play "Imagine" on ukulele while throwing Molotov cocktail

"Imagine there's more riots . . ."

Distract cops with Krispy Kreme while friend steals LEGO set

If you can get the $800 Millennium Falcon, you are legally skilled.

Challenge cops to *Super Smash Bros.*

Fox-only, No Items, Final Destination

MOST TERRIFYING CRIMINALS FROM
THE JANUARY 6 INSURRECTION

Here are the nine most terrifying criminals from that dark day of January 6, 2021—a day that will live in infamy:

Buffalo Guy

Look at this face: truly terrifying. Legal experts all agree that since he stood up in front of the congressional chambers, he is now legally our ruler. Bow down before Buffalo Guy!

Knittin' MeeMaw Gunderson

Wow. Terror. Horror. Truly the face of a criminal. OK, technically she was storming the Kansas state capitol and not the one in D.C., but still—she's such a terrorist that her terror spreads across the whole land.

The guy who put his feet on Pelosi's desk

The act of a madman. The nation will never recover.
THAT IS MAHOGANY!

The massive army of robot assassins who literally murdered AOC

These guys were ruthless. RIP, AOC. Fs in the chat for the world's smartest socialist.

The deadly lectern thief

Whole chapters in future history textbooks will be written about this guy, who literally walked into the building and walked out with a piece of wood. We're talking John Wilkes Booth levels of impact on our country.

This squirrel

Just look at him. He's clearly up to something.

MOST TERRIFYING CRIMINALS FROM
THE JANUARY 6 INSURRECTION (CONTINUED)

This pigeon

Dastardly.

These professional insurrectionists who were having quite a bit of trouble climbing a wall

Had they succeeded in climbing the wall, the law of the land would have mandated that we make them our rulers. They would have had to fight Buffalo Guy in unarmed combat for the honor, though.

And the mastermind behind it all:

This deranged lunatic who specifically told everyone to remain peaceful

This psycho said, "I know that everyone here will soon be marching over to the Capitol building to peacefully and patriotically make your voices heard."

Truly the rallying cry of a madman.

We know these pictures are hard to look at. But it's important to remember how terrible this day was so we will never repeat it.

THE MOST PEACEFUL PROTESTERS OF ALL TIME

Here are the nine most peaceful protesters we've ever seen from the left.

Just bask in the peace!

This lady (?) screaming at the sky

Look at the peace on her (?) face—the love. The tolerance. The pure, unadulterated, self-righteous bliss. So peaceful.

This guy kicking a pro-lifer

There's no better way to show how peaceful you are than to kick a pro-lifer. She's pro-life, so she was really asking for it.

This woman stealing an entire Cheesecake from the Cheesecake Factory

Stick it to Big Cheesecake.

This guy celebrating the arson of an Arby's

Is there anything more peaceful than burning down the home of the classic, slow-roasted beef and cheddar sandwich? Arby's: they'll no longer have the meats when Antifa is through with them. ('Cause, you know, they're burned to the ground.)

This based dude dragging a whole ATM onto a public bus

Just live your truth, based ATM guy. Live. Your. Truth.

THE MOST PEACEFUL PROTESTERS OF ALL TIME (CONTINUED)

This squirrel throwing a Molotov cocktail at an old lady

We always knew the squirrels were up to something.

The protesters who spelled out the word "LOVE" with burning buildings

Now even the space aliens will know that this protest is about love. <3

This sitting congresswoman riling up a crowd to assault Trump supporters in public

You can feel the peace and harmony oozing from Maxine Waters's every move. Now she's making good trouble!

And the mastermind behind it all:

Famed lizard person: GEORGE SOROS

Well, he certainly looks peaceful now that he's gotten the masses to all fight amongst themselves.

Let them eat cake peacefully!

Mostly.

IT'S YOUR DEMOCRACY: PARTICIPATE!

Whether you choose to participate in our democracy with insurrections or peaceful protests, it's essential that you jump in there and get involved.

Read on, fellow lover of democracy, for some handy tips on how to DESTROY those who disagree with you.

It's the only way for our society to survive.

CHAPTER REVIEW: INSURRECTIONS AND (MOSTLY) PEACEFUL PROTESTS

We've discussed so many incredible things in these last few pages. Let's take a minute to check our comprehension for absolutely no reason whatsoever.

1. Are you more of an insurrectionist or a peaceful protester?

2. If you had to throw one object at a political opponent, what would it be?

3. How did the gavel feel? Describe the texture.

4. Thomas Jefferson once said, "The tree of liberty must be refreshed from time to time with the blood of patriots and tyrants. It is its natural manure." This sort of revolutionary spirit seemed to kindle in a reign of terror in France, against which Edmund Burke took his pen, warning, "Rage and frenzy will pull down more in half an hour, than prudence, deliberation, and foresight can build up in a hundred years" while suggesting, "a state without the means of some change is without the means of its conservation." In the space provided, please analyze the parable of G. K. Chesterton's Fence and ask yourself if some abstract rights of man promoted by the likes of Thomas Paine are the correct foundation for a stable system of government.

5. What is the insurrection in your life that you need to give over to God?

6. Would you rather fight one hundred Ben Shapiro–sized insurrectionists or one insurrection-sized Ben Shapiro?

Chapter 10

Destroying Your Political Opponents' Stupid Faces

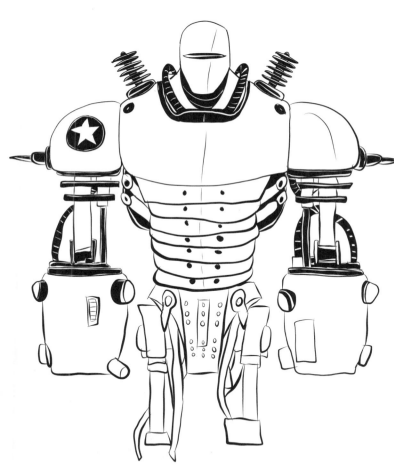

"DEATH IS A PREFERABLE ALTERNATIVE TO COMMUNISM!"
LIBERTY PRIME is a great example of how to destroy your opponents.
Be like LIBERTY PRIME.

Our country is deeply **divided.** It's important that we heal those divides by utterly destroying our political opponents' stupid faces so that only our own political views will remain! No more division!

Some people will tell you we should be kind and civil to everyone. You should immediately punch those people in the face, because they don't know what they're talking about.

If you want peace and unity, it's important to

OWN,
DESTROY, and
CRUSH

your enemies and salt the earth where they once stood. Then you should upload a video of you obliterating them to inspire more worthy soldiers to your cause.

TO WAR!!!!

"What is best in life is to crush your enemies, see them driven before you, and hear the lamentations of their Twitter Stans."

—*Conan the Barbarian*

THE TRUE NATURE OF YOUR ENEMY

If you want to be ready to crush those who don't agree with you into a fine power and spread their dumb, stupid ashes on the wind, you need to remind yourself how bad and ugly and evil they really are.

Some people will tell you to assume the best about your political opponents. This is likely because your political opponents have brainwashed them with their evil political-opponent dark magic. Such people are not to be trusted.

Things people might tell you about your political opponents:

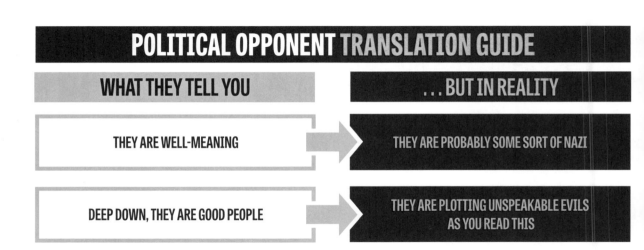

POLITICAL OPPONENT TRANSLATION GUIDE

WHAT THEY TELL YOU	...BUT IN REALITY
THEY ARE WELL-MEANING	THEY ARE PROBABLY SOME SORT OF NAZI
DEEP DOWN, THEY ARE GOOD PEOPLE	THEY ARE PLOTTING UNSPEAKABLE EVILS AS YOU READ THIS

POLITICAL OPPONENT TRANSLATION GUIDE

WHAT THEY TELL YOU	...BUT IN REALITY
WHILE NOT PERFECT, THEY DO HAVE SOME VALID ARGUMENTS	THEY HAVE REALLY BAD BREATH
THEY HAVE A LOVING RELATIONSHIP WITH THEIR KIDS	THEY NEVER BRING THE SHOPPING CARTS BACK TO THE CORRAL WHEN THEY'RE DONE
THEY'RE GOOD WITH ANIMALS	THEY ARE STUPID NITWITS WITH VERY TINY LITTLE NITWIT BRAINS
THEY CAN KNIT A FANTASTIC SCARF	THEY ARE UGLY
THEIR HOME-BREWED IPA IS TO DIE FOR	THEY ARE MAYBE CREEPY RAPISTS OR SOMETHING. YIKES!
THEY JUST WANT EVERYONE TO BE HAPPY	THEY EAT PINEAPPLE PIZZA—WITH A FORK—AFTER DABBING IT WITH A PAPER TOWEL
THEY'RE DOING THE BEST THEY CAN	THEY HATE CHILDREN
THEY HAVE HOPES, DREAMS, AND HIDDEN TALENTS	THEY TEXT AND DRIVE WHILE VAPING AND LISTENING TO NICKELBACK
THEY ARE VALUABLE INDIVIDUALS ENTITLED TO DIGNITY AND RESPECT	THEY WILL DESTROY THIS COUNTRY AND EVERYTHING YOU HOLD DEAR UNLESS YOU DESTROY THEM **RIGHT NOW**

Now that you know the true nature of your irredeemable wicked enemies, it's time to

GET PUMPED UP

for glorious combat with the forces of political wickedness!

Once you're ready for battle, it's time to choose the field on which you will engage your enemies. Whether you're on social media, at the Thanksgiving dinner table, in the halls of Congress, or meeting your enemies face-to-face in the streets, here's everything you need to to win your battle of ideas against your dum-dum-head opponents!

SOCIAL MEDIA **WARS**

There is a time and place for all things under the sun. You may occasionally disagree with a friend or relative over a minute policy issue, and wonder how best to approach it. You could try gently pulling them aside in person and asking how they came to a certain conclusion on a given subject, or you could go about things the right way and berate them in a Facebook post where they will read any potential nuance in tone as passive aggression.

The added benefit is it allows all of your mutual friends and family to bear witness to the awesome might of your intellectual firepower as you pulverize Aunt Mabel for her stupid opinion on veganism. The icing on the cake is that while your soul atrophies and your empathy for humankind slowly diminishes, you're also making Mark Zuckerberg cold, hard cash!

Contrary to popular belief, you do not need any facts or statistics to win internet arguments.

Here are a few general strategies you can implement to throw your intellectual opposition for a loop:

HOW TO WIN AN ARGUMENT ON SOCIAL MEDIA

Call them racist
If you call them a racist every time they make a good point, they will constantly be on the defensive.

Post a link to a website with a clickbait title
The post will only seem to corroborate the point you're trying to make. You don't even have to read the contents of the article, because they definitely won't either.

Click on the handy-dandy "send mob" button
to summon an army of rabid, emotionally disturbed social media zombie warriors to your cause.

Tag their family members in your replies
This will bring additional shame on them.

Tag their employer or business partners in arguments
This will destroy their livelihoods and their very ability to feed their families. That'll learn 'em! And their families.

Make fun of their profile picture
If they are especially stupid-looking, just repost a picture of their face and say "no comment." DESTROYED.

Make vague claims
Tell them, "I don't have time to explain this to you, but you can look it up for yourself. DO THE WORK!"

Remind them of your prestigious academic qualifications
Because poli-sci majors are better people than most.

Create a secondary burner account
It will come to your defense in whatever argument you're trying to win.

PRO TIP REMEMBER TO HAVE FUN!
The fact that you're destroying relationships and widening the chasm currently rending our political landscape doesn't mean you can't also find enjoyment in the downfall of humanity!

THE BATTLE OF WASHINGTON, D.C.

Only the most valiant political warriors are chosen to compete in the bloody gladiatorial combat of D.C. as elected representatives. If you are one of the brave, fortunate few chosen for this glorious purpose, you will need to prepare. It's important, first of all, to leave your conscience, your moral compass, and your very soul behind. These will only hinder your ability to win. Only after you have been completely hollowed of all positive human social traits are you ready to fight. Also, it helps if you have really good hair and straight teeth. Then, imbued with the power of dark money and Deep State corruption, you will be able to face the enemies of all that is pure and good according to your political leanings. You will also be able to make a ton of money and speak on cable news and stuff—it's a perk.

HOW TO PREVAIL IN GLORIOUS COMBAT FOR WASHINGTON, D.C.

Here are the time-honored techniques you should be familiar with to win as an elected politician. If you find your conscience disturbed by any of these techniques, you need to go find yourself a red-hot iron poker and sear that conscience a little more until it's well-done. Then get back in there, tiger!

Call your opponent a racist. Yes, this is a social media technique that works even better in real life. Then, make a few commercials about how your opponent is racist.

Ask the Russians to write up a dossier with all kinds of salacious material to smear your opponents' reputations. If you don't know any Russians, write a dossier yourself and send it to Buzzfeed. They'll publish literally anything.

Send the dossier to the FBI, so it'll have an excuse to wiretap your opponents' phones, hack their computers, subpoena all their friends and family, and throw them in jail. BRUTAL!

Drone strike them. Easy peazy.

Tell them you will vote against their the line item in their spending bill that funds a giant bridge with a bronze likeness of their face on it. One of the most hurtful things you can do.

Literally kill them. There are so many great assassin services in D.C., so we hear.

Have a televised debate in which both sides can be heard so that people can come to their own conclusions. LOL just kidding.

Have a televised shouting match where you one-up each other with practiced zingers and talking points so everyone can see what a loser your opponent is.

Ask the press to smear your opponents on the evening news for you, leaving you above the fray. Just look at you up there, above the fray! So dignified!

OWNING YOUR STUPID RELATIVES AT THANKSGIVING

One of America's most beloved traditions is sitting down with family at Thanksgiving to share a meal, reflecting on all the blessings you've been given . . .

CONSERVATIVE HOUSEHOLDS

1. DRESS THE TURKEY IN A MAGA HAT. Carefully dress the turkey. Not the regular kind of dressing; dress it in a MAGA hat. It will have the added benefit of triggering your stupid liberal nephew.

2. COSPLAY AS PRESIDENT TRUMP. Dust off your authentic President Trump cosplay outfit and get ready to watch your lib relatives LITERALLY DIE when you open the door to greet them. Classic!

3. INVITE BEN SHAPIRO TO SPEAK. "OK folks, who made the cranberries?" While everyone's sitting down to a nice meal without controversy, you dim the lights. You ask everyone to welcome the guest speaker: Ben freakin' Shapiro! As Ben begins to rattle off FACTS and LOGIC, you can kick back as your lib relatives' heads literally explode.

4. SAY A TOUCHING, HEARTFELT PRAYER FOR THE MEAL, AND THEN CARVE THE TURKEY WITH AN AR-15. After a moment of unity in prayer, pull down the ceremonial AR-15 hanging above your kitchen sink and carve that turkey with a full magazine of ammo.

5. LOUDLY SING "GOD BLESS AMERICA" AS YOU WELCOME THEM INTO YOUR HOME. When you open the door and they say, "Happy Thanksgiving!" just blast 'em with the entire song in the original language: AMERICAN.

6. WHENEVER ONE OF YOUR LIBTARD RELATIVES EXPRESSES AN EMOTION, JUMP ALL UP IN THEIR FACE AND SHOUT, "FACTS DON'T CARE ABOUT YOUR FEELINGS!" If someone says, "Man, I'm feeling tired" or "Boy, do I feel full!" stop what you're doing, leap across the room and shout, "FACTS DON'T CARE ABOUT YOUR FEELINGS, SNOWFLAKE!" They'll probably ask for a safe space after that, are we right or are we right?

7. HAND OUT GIFT BAGS WITH A FREE ASSAULT RIFLE, A BIBLE, AND A TRUMPY BEAR. As everyone's leaving your home, pass out some memorable gift bags. Their new memorabilia will either melt their faces off or turn them into a real American at long last.

. . . and then mercilessly PWNing them at the dinner table for their stupid freaking opinions. Here is how to own your relatives at Thanksgiving, whether you're in a conservative household or a liberal one:

LIBERAL HOUSEHOLDS

1. Make everyone kneel down before your "In this house, we believe" sign.

2. Everyone must kiss your George Floyd statue before they get stuffing.

3. Pass out pride-themed COVID masks everyone is required to wear.

4. Play Yoko Ono music the entire time.

5. Everyone must submit to a temperature check and an anal COVID swab test.

6. If anyone tries to say a prayer of thanks, scream, "THERE IS NO GOD!" and throw a turkey leg at them

7. Mix in some puberty blockers with the mashed potatoes.

8. Lay a rainbow flag on the table. Uncle Walt will be so triggered!

9. Cook a vegan tofu turkey and watch Aunt Binny grimace while she eats it. LOL!

10. Open dinner with a thirty-minute acknowledgement that the dining room in which you're sitting rests on unconceded indigenous lands and then say a blessing to the Great Spirit in the original Cherokee.

FIGHT YOUR POLITICAL OPPONENTS THE CIVILIZED WAY:
WITH A GOOD, OLD-FASHIONED DUEL

Nowadays we are fully enlightened beings, able to fight with just our words, cutting remarks, ad hominem attacks, libelous statements, and reputation-annihilating accusations. However, back in the primitive olden days, words were cheap, so people fought with weapons. We all know about Aaron Burr and Alexander Hamilton, but there are so many others who were forced to throw away their shot.

If it comes to it, you may need to settle your disagreement with a good, old-fashioned duel. We do not condone this practice in any way, but if you do, please remember to get it on video—and hold the camera in landscape mode, for goodness sake.

Here are some famous duels from political history:

A DUEL TO REMEMBER

Abraham Lincoln dueled Edward Cullen for the fate of the Union

When Lincoln saw Cullen glistening in the sunlight, he realized Edward wasn't a real vampire, and thus withdrew from the duel.

Obi-Wan Kenobi dueled Anakin Skywalker for the fate of the Galactic Republic

In this fiery duel, Obi-Wan underestimated Anakin's power, but wisely took the high ground.

Yugi Mutou famously dueled Atem with his *Yu-Gi-Oh!* cards

In the end, both were destroyed with 200 life points apiece.

A DUEL TO REMEMBER (CONTINUED)

George Washington dueled King George in a glove-slap battle

King George famously lost and decided to start the Revolutionary War as revenge.

Alexander Hamilton dueled Aaron Burr

Actually, it was more of a rap battle, but Aaron Burr rapped so well that it literally killed Hamilton. Sad!

John Wayne dueled Barack Obama

It was high noon, and it was for the fate of America. Wayne lost. Oh no!

Elon Musk challenged Vladimir Putin

Format: Single combat
Stakes: Freedom of Ukraine
Putin: Chickened out

Bonesaw wrassled that no-good, lyin', cheatin' Peter Parker

Spider-Man had powers, but didn't disclose them. If he didn't have them, Bonesaw would've crushed him. BONESAWWWW!!!!!

POLITICAL FISTICUFFS: COMBAT MOVES TO TAKE DOWN THOSE

HOW TO DESTROY A REPUBLICAN

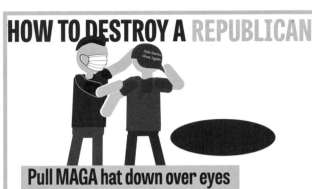

Pull MAGA hat down over eyes

Coax into an open manhole while yelling, "HOW CAN YOU BE SO BLIND?"

Shout Your Non-Binary Pronouns

Ze/Zir/Zoo! Don't be afraid to make up a few!

HOW TO DESTROY A DEMOCRAT

Hold up a copy of Constitution

This will instantly limit their governing authority.

Shout "There are only TWO genders!"

They will cower before your bountiful knowledge of the human reproductive system.

HOW TO DESTROY A LIBERTARIAN

Say you're from the IRS

"Sir, you are now responsible for the entire national debt." Add some clip-on ties to complete the look.

Ask "Who will build the roads?"

Ask who will build roads if the government doesn't. They have definitely never considered that, ever.

ON THE WRONG SIDE OF HISTORY

These moves have been passed down over generations. Learn each one and destroy your enemy.

Hire Nicolas Cage to steal Constitution

In addition, destroy the 2nd Amendment

Distract with Ben Shapiro videos

Then drop a piano on head

Lure to open sand

Use a "FREE MONEY FROM GOVERNMENT" sign and cackle as sandworm eats them.

Distract with Obama videos

Then drop a piano on head

Lure them in with Rush's *2112*

While they're distracted by that sweet vinyl, handcuff them to water heater.

Distract with Ron Paul videos

Then drop a piano on head

POLITICAL FISTICUFFS: COMBAT MOVES TO TAKE DOWN THOSE

HOW TO DESTROY A REPUBLICAN

Slightly criticize President Trump

"Did you know that Donald Trump eats his steak well-done with a side of ketchup?"

Sabotage Goya beans

Sneak giant ghost pepper into their Goya beans

HOW TO DESTROY A DEMOCRAT

Deploy boom box with Rush Limbaugh

Play all of his greatest hits—letting loose curses on all liberals

Ask "What is a woman?"

Democrats don't understand simple scientific questions.

HOW TO DESTROY A LIBERTARIAN

Lace their drugs with laxatives

Maybe that'll teach them to "just say no" to drugs and alcohol abuse.

Get them to invest in Nigerian Bitcoin

Fool them with a Nigerian prince Bitcoin scam. Fortune favors the bold!

ON THE WRONG SIDE OF HISTORY (CONTINUED)

Hide scorpions in their MyPillow

That'll teach them to advocate for personal liberty! What a dummy! HAHAHA!

Gavel bop

Lay down the law with Justice Sonia Sotomayor's supreme gavel . . . Hey, where'd you get that?

Tatsumaki Senpukyaku

Execute a flawless hurricane kick while shouting, "TRUMP WON!"

Summon terrifying angel from Ezekiel

The angel will tell them scary things like, "Be not afraid" and "Jesus wasn't a socialist."

Fill their AR-15 with harmless Jell-O

Who are they going to complain to, the government? Time to do Jell-O shots!

Hide bees in their fedora

OH, NO, NOT THE BEES! NOT THE BEES! AAAAHHHH!! OH, THEY'RE IN MY EYES! MY EYES! AAAAGGGHHH!!!

YOU ARE THE POLITICS CHAMPION

Your political opponents have been thoroughly destroyed. Through your unassailable arguments, impeccable logic, incredible good looks, and raw masculine energy, the enemies on the other side of the aisle have been crushed. We can hear the lamentations of their women from here.

Great job! You're going to make a great participant in democracy. As your enemies writhe beneath your foot, bruised and bloodied from the curb-stomping you gave them, they'll have plenty of time to think about how right your position is.

And maybe, just maybe, one day you can be friends. But until that day, just keep on crushing them.

For you are the champion, our friend.

CHAPTER REVIEW: DESTROYING YOUR POLITICAL OPPONENTS' STUPID FACES

We've discussed so many incredible things in these last few pages. Let's take a minute to check our comprehension for absolutely no reason whatsoever.

1. Whom do you wish to destroy? Write their name(s) below.

2. What method would you use to destroy them? Please be detailed.

3. Do you know where I can buy a new gavel? **Someone** *ruined the last one we had.*

4. Would you come on down to the station and answer a few questions for us?

5. Ever since John Locke and the Enlightenment-era development of what has come to be known as classical liberalism, freedom of speech and tolerance of others' ideas have been assumed to be the foundation for the entire structure of our pluralistic system of government. Dr. Ron Paul said, "We don't have freedom of speech to talk about the weather. We have the First Amendment so we can say very controversial things." In the space provided, please list all your most controversial beliefs and the reasons why your preferred conspiracy theory is absolutely true.

6. Have you ever seen the inside of a Turkish prison?

Chapter 11

Money and Government Spending

Money. **What is it?** Is it good? Some people think so. The government sure tries to get as much of it as possible from you every year, so it might be worth taking a look at the government's relationship with money.

First off, how much money does the government make? If you answered NONE, you'd be right on the money, or more accurately: right on the NOT money. The government doesn't make any money itself, so naturally, it has to take money from you.

How does it do this? By force, of course!

Politicians love to tell their constituents they will be providing useful programs that are compassionate and caring, but they never really like to talk about where the money to fund those programs comes from.

Here's a fun illustration showing how government spending works:

SOCIAL SECURITY

The Social Security Act was signed into law in 1935 by President Franklin D. Roosevelt. Its primary goal was to provide a federal safety net for elderly, retired, and disabled American citizens. FDR initially intended the program to be a temporary measure that would eventually be replaced by private retirement plans, but soon realized that most people are chumps and that he could just perpetually tell them they were entitled to things that only he could provide.

This strategy got him elected president four times.

Brilliant!

Many people don't understand how Social Security works. It's really not all that hard to understand once you see it visualized (Figure 1):

Retirees and those unable to work collect Social Security from the active workforce, and when the active workforce retires, they collect Social Security from the next generation of the workforce. Money just keeps getting shuffled upward, and the new pledges get the privilege of entering this exciting opportunity . . . or face jail time.

This is nothing like Bernie Madoff's Ponzi scheme, as you can clearly see (Figure 2):

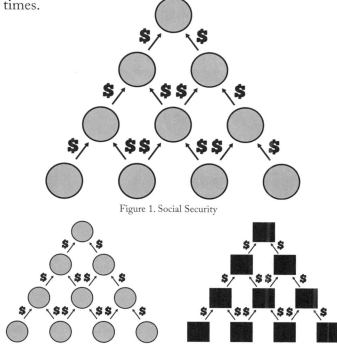

Figure 1. Social Security

Figure 2. Social Security vs Ponzi Scheme

DID YOU KNOW?

Your Social Security money isn't actually saved or invested for future generations. The government just spends the money immediately and replaces it with an **I.O.U.** for future taxpayers to shoulder! **Efficient!**

TIMES ARE TOUGH... HERE'S SOME MONEY

As our government continues to take our money and we spiral into an endless vortex of fiscal misery, there may be occasions when you don't have any financial means of providing sustenance for your children. We understand and are here for you.

On this page, you'll find two fully paper bills that do not actually act as legal tender, but if you distract a cashier sufficiently while handing him one of these, it's possible he won't notice.

NATIONAL DEBT

As of 2022, the U.S. national debt was over $30 trillion. Written out numerically, that would be $30,000,000,000,000. That's 30 million times a million. The vast majority of us have no idea how to even conceptualize figures that exceed one million, so we've compiled some visualizations to illustrate how much money that is.

$30,000,000,000,000
in $1 Bills (Height)

30 Trillion in $1 Bills = 2,035,984 miles

Distance from Earth to moon = 238,900 miles

Earth's circumference = 24,901 miles

Great Wall of China = 13,171 miles

Distance from the earth to International Space Station = 254 miles

Grand Canyon = 0.4924242 miles

Empire State Building = 0.2753788 miles

Eiffel Tower = 0.2051136 miles

Henry Cavill = 0.001136364 miles

NATIONAL DEBT (CONTINUED)

$30,000,000,000,000

in $1 Bills (Size)

1000 FT.
1000 FT.
1000 FT.

1. International Space Station (357') **2.** Blue whale (79') **3.** *Millenium Falcon* (114')
4. *USS Enterprise* - NCC-1701 (947') **5.** Stack of One Hundred Elephants (1000') **6.** Megazord (333') **7.** The Village People (10 feet, 50 toes)
8. Crypto.com Arena - Filled with Jell-O (The Jell-O is irrelevant to the volume, but it's fun to think about) (764')
9. *USS Midway* (971') **10.** Colosseum (510') **11.** Great Pyramid of Giza (756') **12.** Military spending (295' x 295' x 295')

NATIONAL DEBT (CONTINUED)

66,138,678,655 lbs

$30,000,000,000,000 in $1 Bills (Weight)

*This book was written in 2022. If history is any indicating factor, by the time you read this, the national debt will have increased significantly.

1. 2,252 Brooklyn bridges **2.** 2,966 Eiffel towers **3.** The total weight of vegetables that go bad in your fridge each year
4. 340,921,021 Post Malones and both members of Milli Vanilli **5.** Sack of 22,046,226,218 rabid ferrets (not including the sack)
6. 1,563,562,143 Mjölnirs, none of which you are worthy enough to lift **7.** 3 Nokia 3310s **8.** 6,613,867,865 12-packs of Mountain Dew Code Red
9. 4,219,373 times the weight of Big Macs Don Gorske has eaten **10.** 18,130,120 Tesla Model 3s **11.** 14,697 Space Shuttles **12.** Your mom

GOVERNMENT PROGRAMS

Now that we know what money looks like, it's about time we learned where our tax dollars actually go.

Can you guess which one of these things the government actually funded with your tax money?

HOW DOES THE GOVERNMENT SPEND MY TAXES?

01

- **A** Argentinian clown college
- **B** A study on the proliferation of alcoholism within the gay community
- **C** Crack pipes
- **D** All of the above

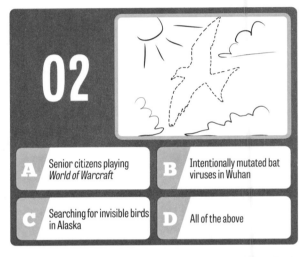

02

- **A** Senior citizens playing *World of Warcraft*
- **B** Intentionally mutated bat viruses in Wuhan
- **C** Searching for invisible birds in Alaska
- **D** All of the above

03

- **A** Providing cocaine to Japanese quail
- **B** Studying whether selfies make people happy
- **C** Sending Pakistani children to a Dolly Parton–themed amusement park
- **D** All of the above

04

- **A** Slot machines for pigeons
- **B** Giving cigarettes to children
- **C** $10 million on soda bottles that served no purpose before being discarded
- **D** All of the above

05

A Attempting to improve the flavor of tomatoes

B Teaching farmers how to use Facebook

C An opera about Prince Harry

D All of the above

06

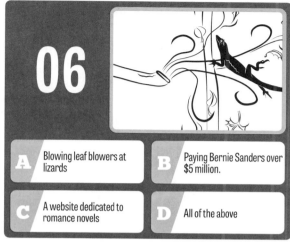

A Blowing leaf blowers at lizards

B Paying Bernie Sanders over $5 million.

C A website dedicated to romance novels

D All of the above

07

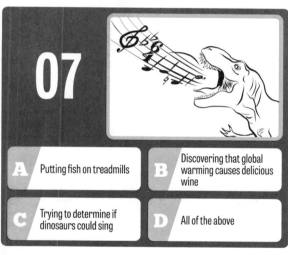

A Putting fish on treadmills

B Discovering that global warming causes delicious wine

C Trying to determine if dinosaurs could sing

D All of the above

08

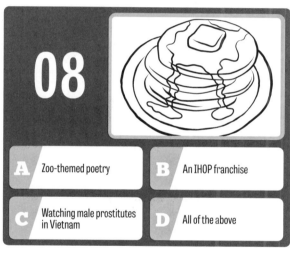

A Zoo-themed poetry

B An IHOP franchise

C Watching male prostitutes in Vietnam

D All of the above

09

A Crushing the skulls of babies

B Crushing the skulls of babies in other countries

C Subsidizing companies that specialize in crushing the skulls of babies

D All of the above

Turn this page over to see the answers!

ANSWERS: D, D, D, D, D

IRS PROS AND CONS

Everything in this wide world exists in a delicate balance. In Newtonian terms: for every action, there is an equal and opposite reaction. A clear illustration of this principle is displayed in the actions of America's first bearded president. Abraham Lincoln played a large role in the freeing of American slaves; however, he also established the Internal Revenue Service, essentially binding all future citizens into another kind of slavery.

Sad.

Some people claim the IRS is a tangled web of intricate traps of obscure legal minutia maliciously designed to wring every last penny from your lifeless hands as its agents cackle maniacally as they adjust their monocles and top hats.

OTHER PEOPLE ARE WRONG.

Here's a breakdown weighing the pros and cons of the IRS.

PROS	CONS
⊘ Caught Al Capone	⊗ Evil
	⊗ Immoral
	⊗ Malicious
	⊗ Greedy
	⊗ Dumb
	⊗ Not Good
	⊗ Worthy of Mockery
	⊗ Downright Unpleasant
	⊗ Wasteful
	⊗ Hasteful
	⊗ Graceful
	⊗ Playskool

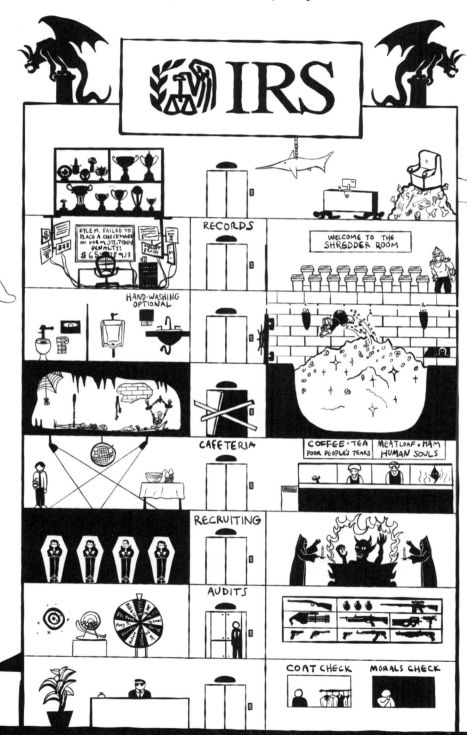

INSIDE THE IRS: A CLOSER LOOK

WHEN DOES THE GOVERNMENT TAX YOU?

As mentioned earlier in this chapter, the government doesn't make any money itself, so it has to dip into your pockets in order to survive. It's our civic duty and responsibility to help keep the wheels turning and to assist in the upkeep of Bernie's three houses and Nancy Pelosi's $24,000 refrigerator.

So when exactly does the government take from us?

The answer is: it taxes us every time we make money, and then every time we so much as look at the money.

Here are a few instances when the government will stick its hands in the ol' coffers.

HOW WILL THE GOVERNMENT TAKE MY MONEY?

Income Tax

Every time you make money, the government will take a slice of the pie.

Payroll Tax

When your employer pays you, the government will swoop in and nab a piece.

Social Security Tax

Regardless of whether you'd benefit from it, the government will demand a ransom here too.

Sales Tax

Whenever you spend your hard-earned previously taxed dollars, the government will say, "More please!"

Capital Gains Tax

If you wisely invest your previously taxed money and turn a profit, the government will request (read: extort) a cut of it.

Property Tax

Own property? The government will hold out a soup bowl and pitifully cry, "Please sir, I want some more."

Inheritance Tax

Great Aunt Dolly passed away and left you some change? The government inherits some as well.

Gift Tax

Want to help out your broke nephew in college? Uncle Sam takes a cut.

Estate Tax

Dead? Taxed.

INFLATION: HOW TO PROTECT YOURSELF

Inflation is the upward movement of prices in goods and services within a given economy. Inflation can occur when:

- Demand for a product exceeds supply
- It costs more than it used to to produce a product
- The government prints money like there's no tomorrow, causing your savings to be worthless.

Scary stuff!

However, there are a few surefire ways to protect yourself against the looming threat of inflation.

SURVIVING INFLATION

Hoard your mint-condition Pokémon cards and Beanie Babies: Experts say these could be the primary currency of our dystopian future! Be sure to hold on to your pogs, slammers, and Funko Pop dolls as well.

Become one of those guys at the beach with a metal detector: Let's be honest: this is the American Dream right here!

"Inflation is as violent as a chuegy mugger, as sus as an armed robber and as deadly as a clapped hit man who would have you catch these hands. Periodt. IYKYK."

—Ronald Reagan
(adapted for 2022)

Become an indentured servant: Learn new skills! Work with your hands! Get stuff in return, like a potato or some gruel!

Collect gold bars: You can melt them down and make high-level gold swords and armor, making you the most powerful fighter so you can steal other people's canned beans.

Allow people to read from your collection of old pre-woke comic books in exchange for goods and services: People will give anything to read the stories from DC and Marvel before they went all "woke" on us.

Sell your least-favorite child: Just don't tell them you're doing it because they're your least favorite or you might hurt their feelings.

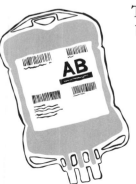

Try to make extra blood plasma: Very lucrative. People always want blood plasma for different stuff and things.

Just "Imagine": Imagine no possessions. It's easy if you try. Imagine there's no Heaven. Imagine all the people living for today! I bet you feel better already!

Put together a raiding party and go raid: As long as you're holding a sign that says "Justice" or something, it should be okay to Leeroy Jenkins to your heart's content.

Exchange work favors, fair and square: Just maybe not with your proctologist.

Just use Chinese yuan: Everyone else will, anyway.

Congratulations!

If you've reached the end of this chapter, you know more about government spending than the average U.S. congressman!

Now you can rest at night knowing your tax dollars are well cared for and the government is really good at spending them efficiently.

CHAPTER REVIEW: MONEY AND GOVERNMENT SPENDING

We've discussed so many incredible things in these last few pages. Let's take a minute to check our comprehension for absolutely no reason whatsoever.

1. How much money do you make?

2. Write your bank account number below for safekeeping.

3. What is the metaphorical government spending in your life that you can give to God?

4. The question of whether or not we should have a central bank or a currency not backed by precious metals goes back to the very beginning of the nation, when Federalists like Alexander Hamilton sought to establish a Bank of the United States and were opposed by Democratic-Republicans like Thomas Jefferson. Andrew Jackson, who killed the second bank of the United States, once said, "If the people only understood the rank injustice of our money and banking system, there would be a revolution by morning." In the space provided, please read a relevant book from Murray Rothbard in order to answer this question: What has government done to our money?

5. No, seriously. Did you touch the gavel?

Chapter 12

A Glossary of
Democracy

So, you've come at long last to the glossary. "Glossary" is a fancy word meaning "list of words with their definite, immutable meanings right beside them, so you won't sound dumb when discussing important topics with your friends." You'd know that if you had ever read a glossary.

But it's never too late to get educated when it comes to politics. If you're ever discussing politics with a friend or mortal enemy and come across a word you don't know, just tell them to hang on a sec while you run home and get your copy of *The Babylon Bee Guide to Democracy*, run back to the spot where you left them, flip to this glossary, and have them stand there awkwardly as they spell the word out slowly so you can look it up. Then you'll sound much smarter for the rest of the conversation!

Best of all, every single definition here has been verified by seventy-nine independent fact-checkers. Not sure what a fact-checker is? You can look it up right here in the glossary. See how handy that is?

Now let's get smart!

America

A nation founded in 1776 by the extremely based George Washington and his friends. God's favorite country.

Bill
A proposal for passing a brand-new law. Requires dollar bills to pass.

Big Tech

One of the main branches of government. Soon to take over all the other branches.

Bipartisanship

LOL

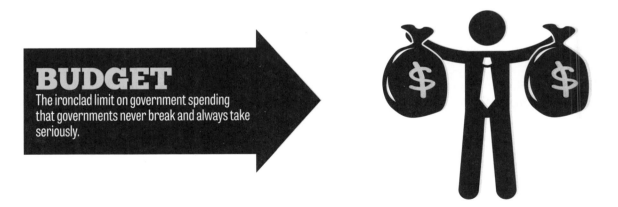

BUDGET
The ironclad limit on government spending that governments never break and always take seriously.

Bureaucrat

A wise and brilliant sage who works tirelessly to keep the many wheels of government turning. It typically takes approximately 32,087 bureaucrats to keep a single part of the government running smoothly. Well, running, anyway.

Capitalism

See "freedom."

Committee

A special group of legislators designed to make it look like legislators actually do something.

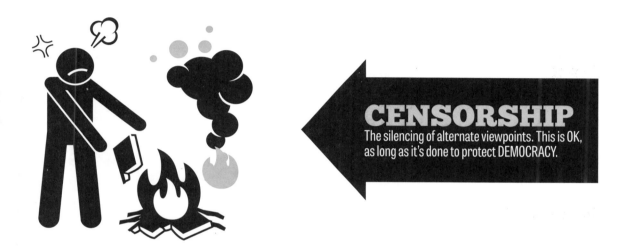

CNN

The nation's most popular, reliable, and trustworthy satire site.

Congress

The highly respected, incorruptible body of legislators that gathers in Washington, D.C., to commit sexual assault and vote themselves pay increases while an authoritarian president makes all the laws. Efficient!

Corruption

When leaders are dishonest and fraudulent for their own benefit. This occurs in the other political party, but never your own.

Corpse

A Democratic voter.

CONSTITUTION

A sacred document first revealed by the Archangel Gabriel and written down by George Washington on golden plates. Reading it out loud has the power to imbue the reader with dangerous levels of freedom.

Debate

A rap battle for old, ugly white people.

Deficit

Spending money that doesn't exist, which is no problem because you can just steal more money from the entire population by printing more money and devaluing the currency! Life hack!

Democracy

A holy institution founded by God Himself and guarded by the *Washington Post*, democracy enables the majority to cruelly enforce their petty will on the minority. Cool.

DUEL *(Yu-Gi-Oh!)*

Ancient Egypt's way of settling disputes by battling for the heart of the cards.

Duel (in politics)

When two politicians used to shoot each other to death. Widely considered to be far more civilized than our political process today.

Electoral College

A constitutional system designed by the Founders to protect us all from democracy.

Fact-Checker

Divine sages gifted to us by the cosmic powers, who reveal all truth. Those who question fact-checkers are enemies of democracy.

Fair Election

An election your side won.

FBI

A well-outfitted standing army stationed in the United States that spies, creates hoaxes, and kills people . . . to protect democracy. Also known as "The Feds."

Federalism

Not sure what this means, but it has the word "Fed" in it so we don't trust it.

FILIBUSTER
A sacred means of safeguarding our democracy from those who wish to destroy it—unless your political rivals use it, in which case it's a wicked tool of oppression used to undermine democracy.

FOREIGN POLICY

A system used to determine which country a president should invade to help his poll numbers.
Usually decided by rolling three dice, as in Risk.

Founding Fathers

A collection of wig-wearing extremists who banded together to invent democracy.

Freedom

A dangerous buzzword weaponized by the Alt-Right to advocate for the ability to do whatever they want. Very undemocratic.

Governor

A mini-president who runs a mini-country called a state.

Hitler

See "Trump."

Human Rights

Some say human rights are inherent and are given by God Himself, which is ridiculous because we all know they are all granted to us by very wise bureaucrats.

Inside Source

A phrase used when reporters just want to write fanfiction about what happened.

Intern

Legalized sex slave for politicians.

IRS
A professional gang of bandits that steals your money in the dead of night to give to bureaucrats so they can maintain the hallowed sanctity of our democracy. Very important!!

Justice

Grouping everyone by class, race, and gender, and treating them all differently based on those categories in order to dismantle systems of cis-white heteronormative patriarchy so we can redistribute wealth, opportunities, and privileges within society so everything is all the same and nothing is ever unfair again and don't worry the bureaucrats will figure all that out if you give them more power they're really smart.

Keynesian Economics

A weird conspiracy theory invented by Paul Krugman while on bath salts.

Law

An important rule written for the benefit of a corporation or the bragging rights of whoever writes and passes the law.

Lobbyist

Person who writes and passes laws.

Legislator

Person paid by lobbyists to pretend he's writing and passing laws.

Magna Carta

The prequel to the Constitution, but not nearly as good.

Meddling in an Election

When Big Tech blocks negative news about their favored candidate and bans anyone who shares it just weeks before the election.

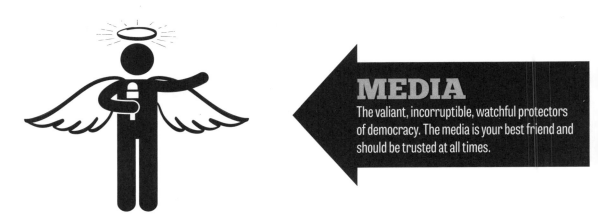

MEDIA
The valiant, incorruptible, watchful protectors of democracy. The media is your best friend and should be trusted at all times.

Medicare

A secret plot by the government to kill all the old people.

Monopoly

A really dangerous concentration of power in one corporate entity. This is really bad except for when the federal government does it.

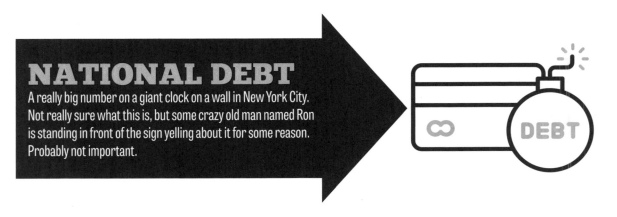

NATIONAL DEBT
A really big number on a giant clock on a wall in New York City. Not really sure what this is, but some crazy old man named Ron is standing in front of the sign yelling about it for some reason. Probably not important.

Nazi

Everyone to the right of Alexandria Ocasio-Cortez.

Oligarchy

Despotic power exercised by a small and privileged group for corrupt or selfish purposes. Wait a minute—is America an oligarchy? We'll get back to you on this.

Politician

An evil race of shape-shifting reptilian humanoids from the Alpha Draconis star system sent here to keep Earthlings under control. Should be kept away from children and small pets at all times.

President

The wise, all-powerful, all-knowing ruler of the land who does whatever he wants via royal decree.

Protest

A way for citizens to make their voices heard when democracy has failed them. Be sure to keep it peaceful by painting "Black Lives Matter" on your sign and throwing Molotov cocktails.

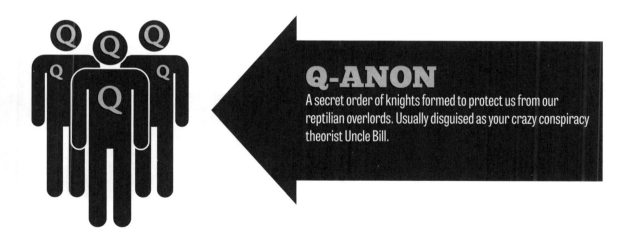

Q-ANON
A secret order of knights formed to protect us from our reptilian overlords. Usually disguised as your crazy conspiracy theorist Uncle Bill.

Representative

An insider trading and sexual harassment connoisseur put in charge of spending your tax dollars. Important!

Rigged Election

An election your side lost.

REPUBLIC

An antiquated system of government once used to rule galaxies from Coruscant until the Jedi Order fell. Not sure who still uses this form of government.

Separation of Church and State

An important legal principle designed to prevent the worship of God from interfering with the worship of government.

SENATOR

One of 100 people who get together in Washington to trade tips on how to treat gout and arthritis.

Separation of Powers

A strategy to limit state power by creating competing power centers. This is fine, as long as they collude once in a while to get things done and oppress the people . . . for DEMOCRACY.

Socialism

Nothing wrong or harmful about this at all, as long as it's DEMOCRATIC socialism.

SUPREME COURT
Like a regular court, but with tomatoes and sour cream. It's also in charge of rubber-stamping tyrannical laws so the government can oppress you legally.

Taxes

Wealth confiscated from private citizens in order to fund the important work of further wealth confiscation.

Trump

See "Hitler."

Tyrant

A really evil dictator—unless he's in your own political party.

Undocumented Immigrant

A Democratic voter.

Unemployment Rate

The number of people in the country ready to be lured into perpetual government dependence by tyrants.

Veto

When the president doesn't like a law, he takes out a giant rubber stamp that says "veto" on it and cancels the law. Most former presidents say this is the most fun aspect of the job.

Vice President

Basically does nothing—a ceremonial position, kind of like the Queen of England.

Vote Harvesting

The practice of driving through heavily Democratic areas in a giant John Deere Vote Combine 9000 and harvesting thousands of votes a minute.

Voting

The most sacred right of any democracy. Should be done en masse by as many uneducated, dumb people as possible.

Welfare

An important means of spreading wealth around the country by robbing everyone who earns it.

WAR
An important means of spreading democracy around the world, by killing everyone who disagrees with it.

White House

A fortified temple of democracy where the High King of Democracy communes with the Dark Powers and sleeps with interns.

Xenophobia

The somewhat justified fear of s***hole countries.

Zahhak

A demonic Persian entity currently running our entire democracy behind the scenes. Creepy!

Afterword

A Final Word

Go Forth and Make Disciples of Democracy

Wow–you made it to the end of the book. Most people don't have the attention span to watch one of those really long sixty-second TikTok videos, so you're head and shoulders above the rest of those dummies.

Great job.

As we close, let's remind ourselves of the lessons we've learned over the last couple hundred pages:

LEARNED LESSONS (CONTINUED)

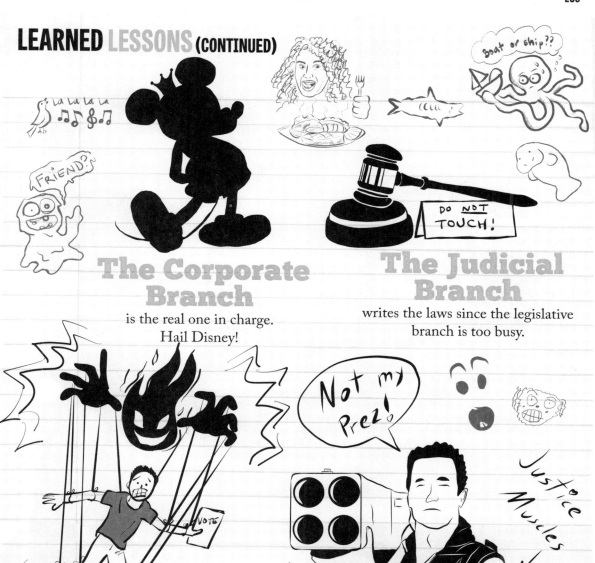

The Corporate Branch

is the real one in charge. Hail Disney!

The Judicial Branch

writes the laws since the legislative branch is too busy.

If you can't win an election, rig it

to be sure your party stays in power forever.

You have constitutional rights

like owning a bazooka and screaming at the sky if you don't like the president.

CONCLUSION

Such powerful lessons to learn!

Now that you have arrived at the peak of the mountaintop of democratic knowledge, it's your duty to go forth and share the information that you've learned with others. Give this book to a friend, or better yet, buy several copies and leave them in public restrooms as though they were Chick tracts. (If you do this, please send us a picture of the books on urinals and such. We would enjoy that immensely.)

In the end, though, the important thing is that we've learned a little something. We've learned that the real destination is the journey. The real America is the friends we make along the way. And the real democracy is inside us all along.

So go forth, faithful soldier of democracy, and **democratize**.

ABOUT THE AUTHORS

Kyle Mann is the editor in chief of The Babylon Bee and coauthor of *How to Be a Perfect Christian*, *The Sacred Texts of The Babylon Bee*, *The Babylon Bee Guide to Wokeness*, and *The Postmodern Pilgrim's Progress*. He lives in the greater San Diego region with his wife, Destiny, and their three boys, Emmett, Samuel, and Calvin. They all voted for Donald Trump seven times.

Joel Berry is the managing editor of The Babylon Bee, coauthor of *The Babylon Bee Guide to Wokeness* and *The Postmodern Pilgrim's Progress*, a columnist, a former worship leader, and a public speaker. He lives with his wife and five crazy kids in northwest Ohio.

Brandon Toy is the director of video production at The Babylon Bee. As a professional videographer of twenty years, it made a lot of sense for him to spend time writing for this book and drawing pictures like a schoolchild. He lives in California with his wife, their cat, and also her cat. He is also Chinese and owns a rice paddy hat, so the picture on the left is not racist.

ABOUT THE ARTISTS

Bettina La Savio is the graphic artist at The Babylon Bee. She dropped out of art school to become a medical professional who tells her coworkers they're all going to get diabetes. She lives in Southern California against her will and hopes to move a less communistic state in the future.

Travis Woodside is a staff writer at The Babylon Bee and failed novelist. He lives in "The Valley" of Southern California with his wife and two daughters. As a member of a Church of Christ, he has developed a severe allergy to instrumental worship and dancing. He acknowledges *The Phantom Menace* as divinely inspired cinema.

Bryan Ming is the other Asian at The Babylon Bee. He showed up one day and was promptly put to work.

ADDITIONAL ART AND DESIGN

Dan Coats   **Emma Spies**   **Gavin Yee**

ACKNOWLEDGEMENTS

Kyle would like to thank his beautiful wife, Destiny, who doesn't think The Babylon Bee is funny but still loves him very much; his kids, Emmett, Calvin, and Samuel; his mom and dad, brother and sisters, and all his extended family who support him and keep subscribing to The Babylon Bee even though he tells them he will give them a free subscription.

Joel would like to thank Seth Dillon, Dan Dillon, and Kyle Mann for building the Bee and giving him the greatest job in the world, his gorgeous wife Kelsey who fills his home with beautiful things and works hard to keep his adorable kids out of his office while he's writing, and his sovereign, faithful, and all-wise Creator.

Brandon would like to first and foremost thank God for the grace, love, and acceptance he doesn't deserve; his wonderful and amazing wife Amy who puts up with all his hijinks; his cousin Ryan; musical partner-in-crime Daniel; Bettina and Travis for going above and beyond their jobs descriptions; Curtis for helping him with math problems for the book; Thomas Sowell, Nicolas Cage, Sizzler, and Terry Crews.

Bettina would like to thank her parents for letting her live in their basement while she shirks her nursing career to draw naked badgers for a living; her kiddos Leela and Zoey for their inspiration and company drawing with her; and her Unk who taught her to sorta care about politics.

Travis would like to thank his even more beautiful wife, Laura, who was patient when he was drawing pictures all weekend instead of spending time with family; his children, Shannon and Lucy, who think the fatter stick figures are funny; and David Duchovny, who is a national treasure. Oh, and his brother Clay, probably.

And we all would like to thank those who have given us so much material to work with:

the United States government, Joe Biden, badgers, George Washington, Abraham Lincoln, Q, Antifa, Brian Stelter, raccoons, squirrels, pigeons, George Lucas, the banana stand, Preston Brooks's cane, the communist country of California, liberals' super-hydrating tears, those goofy libertarians, King George III, AOC's crazy eyes, Donald Trump's regular-sized hands, your mom . . . and the gavel.

THIS IS THE END OF THE BOOK

STOP READING

NO, SERIOUSLY, WHY ARE YOU
STILL READING?

WE WERE VERY CLEAR